APPROACHING FIRE

MICHELLE PORTER

BREAKWATER
P.O. BOX 2188, ST. JOHN'S, NL, CANADA, A1C 6E6
WWW.BREAKWATERBOOKS.COM

A CIP CATALOGUE RECORD FOR THIS BOOK IS AVAILABLE FROM LIBRARY
AND ARCHIVES CANADA

We acknowledge the support of the Canada Council for the Arts. We acknowledge
the financial support of the Government of Canada and the Government of
Newfoundland and Labrador through the Department of Tourism, Culture,
Industry and Innovation for our publishing activities.
PRINTED AND BOUND IN CANADA.

 Canada Council Conseil des arts
for the Arts du Canada
 Canada
Newfoundland
Labrador

Breakwater Books is committed to choosing papers and materials for our
books that help to protect our environment. To this end, this book is
printed on a recycled paper and other controlled sources that are certified
by the Forest Stewardship Council®.

FOR

AMARA, DANNIKA, ELISE AND JASPER,

WITH THE HOPE THAT YOU UNDERSTAND THE STORIES

FROM WHICH ALL OF YOURS BEGAN.

THANK YOU, mama, for reading various drafts and believing in this book. Writing this book and sharing it with you has changed my life. It means so much that you let me get to know our ancestors through all of your stories.

All my thanks and love to auntie Dale for your generosity of spirit and your take-no-holds approach to life and to all the family stories. Thank you for reading drafts of the essay, "Fireweed", that became the foundation of this book and I'm grateful that you answered all my questions. I hope we get to tell stories together soon.

Thank you to the amazing ethnomusicologist Monique Giroux, who generously shared her research with me—and sent me that score she found at the last minute so I could include it in this book and send it to my family.

Thank you to Lisa Bird-Wilson for selecting, editing and publishing the essay, "Fireweed", in the Indigenous Writers and Storytellers issue of Grain in 2019.

Thank you to my cousin Chris for joining me for parts of this journey and for the promise to come along on the next.

I've had two amazing mentors work on different drafts of this book with me. I'd like to extend a big thank you to Katherena Vermette, whose early support, response and edits shaped this book and gave me the confidence to move ahead with it. It was more than amazing to work on the final drafts with Joanne Arnott, whose eye for story and detail made this work better than it was before. The conversations I've had with both of you still guide me. It was an honour to get the chance to work with both of you.

I'd like to thank the Canada Council for the Arts for the funding they provided that supported me through the first draft of this project.

Finally, I'd like to thank my Métis ancestors, whose stories continue to teach me the art of living through difficult times while making music.

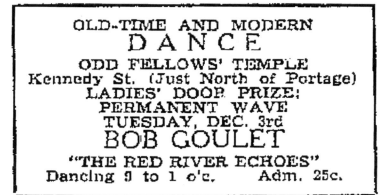

OLD-TIME AND MODERN
DANCE
ODD FELLOWS' TEMPLE
Kennedy St. (Just North of Portage)
LADIES' DOOR PRIZE:
PERMANENT WAVE
TUESDAY, DEC. 3rd
BOB GOULET
"THE RED RIVER ECHOES"
Dancing 9 to 1 o'c.   Adm. 25c.

CONTENTS

PREFACE

My dear Pépé,

I trace you in the stories the women in our family tell, and in the oral family tree shared at all the aunties' kitchen tables, heavy with all the coffees and cookies and bars made of chocolate, icing sugar, and butter. I find pieces of you in the photos and records and official family-tree documents the women kept in their closets to prove who they were, in case anybody asked. You are there in the genealogical book a researcher from La Société historique de Saint-Boniface put together in order to show the breadth and depth of our ancestry in support of my membership with the Manitoba Metis Federation and citizenship with the Métis Nation.

The family tree is not a light document. It has weight. In my hands, it's heavier to pick up than I expected. The family tree exists in two spiral-bound volumes and these pages trace our family back to the time of the voyageurs and the first

French who came to the land we now call Canada. These 200 pages include copies of scrip records I've never seen before. They hold stories that aren't written in the documentation of father, son, uncle and mother, daughter, aunt. The stories are always trying to break away from the plastic coil binding.

You're on the first page of the family tree book. Right there. From my mother to her mother to you, my great-grandfather. Sometimes, the stories I've heard make me forget that I've never met you. I never called you Pépé while you were there across the room, about to look up and see the child asking for your attention.

With each letter, I travel deeper into an old fire started by our ancestors. With each word I place on paper, I am looking for you. I am looking to understand your place in the Métis Nation, and my place as your relation. I write to understand the story of our belonging to each other. Writing is a way of calling out to you.

We never belonged to each other in the way grandparents sometimes belong to their grandchildren; you never fried pancakes for me the way you did for my mother and you never played fiddle in any kitchen I danced in. You were gone before I was born. Yet, each time I find some new detail about your life, the thread that pulls between now and back then gets tangled up in the wings of an emotion I can't name and it takes days to unravel.

Maybe you could help? Oh, laugh and have fun at my expense: I'm not really expecting a voice from the spirit world. But you could answer in the bits and pieces of history that I uncover and weave together here. There is this, too: If I learn to listen in the way that this story needs, you'll keep answering after this book is published. This story we are telling will never be finished and it will be told again and again with beginnings and endings that shift, that change shape.

What I am doing reaches into my college days, when every writing assignment somehow took me back to my grandmother and to you. It reaches into childhood, too, where every story carried a version of your name.

I didn't know all your names then. Knowing you as Pépé, I knew you as a child knows. When I was old enough to know you had a name of your own, I knew you also as Bob and the possibilities of you doubled.

Your full name in our genealogical records: Léon Joseph Robert Goulet.

This name doesn't fit on my tongue. Your recorded birth name is a shirt that is too tight around the shoulders. Everyone called you Bob. The name on most of the vinyl records that keep your songs alive is Bob Goulet. The name used in newspaper advertisements for your performances is Bob Goulet. Who is this Léon Joseph Robert Goulet?

Are you wondering what else I'm going to ask of you? I would, if I were you. If some future great-granddaughter of mine started digging around my life and asking questions, I'd raise an eyebrow. From wherever I was in the afterlife, I'd stop what I was doing and I'd ask if she has any idea what it is she's looking for. By then, I'd know that most of the people who dig for roots in the dirt of their beginnings don't expect to find a sky beneath it all.

Curiosity started it all. All my life I wanted to know why you—great-grandfather, Pépé, Bob—moved away from Manitoba. It was where your music was born; it was where all your relations lived. You left the Métis heartland for the woods of British Columbia, where nobody knew you or your wife or your daughters. I couldn't understand it. I mean, look at where I established my Métis membership: In Manitoba, a place I never lived or even went to growing up. I grew up in Alberta. Many of my cousins and relations live in British Columbia, but Manitoba is where my roots are.

These letters are a beginning. These are the words that have been travelling between my head and my heart. I asked and answers began to arrive. Not always direct ones, but hints and suppositions and maybes. At the end of that I came to the question I think I was really after: How do we belong to each other, my great-grandfather, and what can we teach each other—what can you teach me? This is a beginning.

DISTRIBUTION OF HALF-BREED SCRIP.

Fred. J. Hosken begs to notify persons desirous of purchasing Half-Breed Scrip (which will entitle the holder to 160 acres of land in the Province of Manitoba) that he will be very shortly in a position to supply any quantity of it at the most reasonable terms. Intending purchasers should communicate with him at once.

Radio Programmes

THURSDAY

CKY, WINNIPEG (780)

(CRC)

A.M.
8.30—Opening grain report.
10.30—Mid-session market prices.
11.45—Allan Caron, organist.

P.M.
12.25—"Dorothy."
12.30—Closing grain quotations.
1.15—Livestock report.
(Silent 2 to 4.30)
4.30—Feature Race at Whittier Park.
5.00—Uncle Peter.
6.00—Mrs. David Edwards, contralto;
Gladys Miller, pianist.
6.15—Eric Greenlaw's Harmonicans; Tony
and his Shadow.
6.30—Pleasing Ballads: Wilford Davidson.
6.45—The Fusbys.
7.00—Musicale.
7.15—Connie and Company.
7.25—News bulletins.
7.30—Mid-week Musicale (Ottawa).
8.00—Parade of the Provinces.
8.30—Jasper Park Lodge orch.
9.00—Old Time Frolic.
9.30—News bulletins and weather reports.
9.35—Joe Haymes orch. (CBS).
9.45—Henry Russe's orch. (CBS).
10.00—Prairie Pastoral.
10.30—Red River Echoes: Bob Goulet.
10.45—Hazel McDonald, pianist; Zoe Dee,
popular singer.

10.30—Dancing in the Twin Cities.
11.00—Piano Moods.
11.15—Clyde Lucas' orch.
11.30—Don Pedro orch.

NATIONAL NETWORKS (NBC)

P.M.
7.00—Captain Henry's Show Boat, KFI,
WMAQ, WOC, KOA. (WLW at 7.30).
—Death Valley Days, WLS, WHAM.
WLW.
7.30—George Hessberger Bavarian orch.,
WLS, WHAM, WJR.
8.00—Paul Whiteman's Music Hall Hour.
KFYR, WLW, WOC, WTAM, WFAA.
KOA, KFI.
—Parade of the Provinces, WENR.
WHAM, WJR.
8.30—Echoes of the Palisades, WHAM.
WHAM, WJR.
9.00—Frank Buck, KOA, WFAA, WSM.
9.15—Gene and Glenn: Comedy. WOC,
WMAQ, WSM, KOA, WFI.
—Don Bestor orch., WENR, WJR,
WHAM.
9.30—Bert Block orch., WOC, WTAM.
WMAQ.
—Charlie Davis orch., WHAM, KOA,
WJR, KFYR.
10.00—Milwaukee Philharmonic orch.,
KFYR, WHAM, WJR.
—Mills Blue Rhythm band, WOC,
WTAM, WMAQ.
10.30—Dancing in the Twin Cities, KFYR,
WHAM.
—Shep Fields orch., WOC, WTAM.
WMAQ, WLW.

ONE

Just now it strikes me how easy a thing it is
to misplace a man.

> A woman of course was never difficult
> to misplace.   Women are
> misplaced all the time and
> other than one or two or three lists
> of exceptions
> they aren't much missed
> by the world.

> The gaps where women have been
> filled with something else.
> The shadows
> they leave behind
> swept into dark corners
> basements   places few want
> to look anyway.

But a man? How is he misplaced?

I've been looking for my great-grandfather
Métis fiddler and performer Léon Robert Goulet

He's not a worn nub of a pencil I stopped using.
I didn't leave him in a drawer one day forgotten
after clearing my desk in a hurry because
the children were tumbling
through the door with their friends.

It's not as though I stashed him in the back of the cupboard
for safekeeping
or for the day my schedule would clear up
and incessant chatter took itself out for a bit
left the house

I never had Bob Goulet in the first place.
Except in stories.

Must be late 1950s when the relation they all call
Aunt Lilian is asked to come
to the house in Mission, BC.

She comes
all the way from Winnipeg, Manitoba,
all the way from the Red River, their Métis homeland.

She's there to help with the seven children

Smoke. The kind that's an indicator of a toxic environment or an emotional entanglement that will go bad. There's a spark that might jump across defences and start the kind of fire I haven't experienced since I was a child. There is smoke rising, the tight twist of white in my solar plexus. This smoke is not out there; no, this is the smell of unease in the home of the body that precedes the breaking of a memory, anticipates a blade opening the bowels of the self. Where is the smoke coming from? Will its source come toward me, head this way? Recognize the early signs of danger and learn to write your name, the name you were told was yours. Change course, avoid threat. I know how not to feed a smoulder, how to get out of the way of a lick of heat.

Histories blur and converge in this smoke. I'm reading an oral history-based memoir of my great-great-grandfather's brother's life growing up on the plains and he tells of this summer where there are fires everywhere. His name is Louis Goulet. He is about nine years old and he is travelling with his parents with an organized caravan of Métis families in search of buffalo. His memories in his own words, as collected by Guillame Charette and translated by Ray Ellenwood:

"By the time we got to Beaver River we were already worried about prairie fires cutting into the grazing land we needed along the way, so we veered off a little in the direction of Moose Jaw... After about a week of slow and difficult marching, the smoke rose, indicating either that the fire was no longer in the peat or that the wind had changed direction.... Our guess was soon confirmed."

Seems like the world's on fire, like
the world is just burning itself up.

Music can leap through generations
like fire leaps a road, can't it?

Make itself heard in the cellular activity
of the body of the woman who is standing
in her mother's cousin's kitchen near Mission
the year British Columbia declared a state of emergency.

It's because of all the burning
that didn't happen before and
because of all the fires
that were suppressed—
this music will be felt in the body
of the woman in her kitchen
in her own house
in Newfoundland and Labrador
for years after.

The smoke from those fires travelled.
Filled the skies from the West Coast
to Saskatchewan, and even further east, they say.
When British Columbia burned, smoke made twilight
out of day. In the pictures I saw, I thought
how it could have been fog,

like the clouds that come down to the rocks
in Newfoundland and Labrador
where I make my home.
But the clouds in the pictures billowed
up from the ground
stalked by scathing heat and licking flame.

Standing in my great aunt's kitchen
just a few weeks after the state of emergency lifted
I held in my hands the old brittle records, 78s
coated with shellac resin.
The record covers bear handwritten notes
the names of my great-grandfather and his two daughters
Leon Robert Goulet
        Estelle Rose Goulet, Olive Elise Goulet

My dear Pépé,

What would you say if I told you that Jean Teillet, the great-grandniece of Louis Riel, wrote that the boundaries of the Métis Nation have always been more social than geographic? From the life you knew with your fiddle in Manitoba in the 1930s to the woods in BC for the rest of your life, would you have said that was the way it was for your relations? When your granddaughters—my mom and aunties—talk about you, they share the stories you created, not only the ones you told around the table in the evening, not only the stories in your fiddling and dancing, but also in the stories that told themselves in the life you chose to live.

The Métis Nation, Teillet wrote, traces its identity through their historical stories. From where I am now in time, living somehow or other on a piece of land called Newfoundland and looking back to the stories from the West, I do feel this. The mother-land stolen away from beneath our feet, beneath your feet, Pépé, so many of us pushed off almost every piece of land we tried to call home after that. Didn't matter much how our relations were arranged on the family tree, Cree, English, French, Scottish, Ojibwa, we moved on again and again and everywhere we went we told our stories over and over. You moved on too. You moved with your wife and your daughters from Manitoba to the West Coast. Does this make you a part of the story that Teillet describes?

It's what people pushed to the margins have always done, found life and continuity in their stories. Denied a land base of our own, you built a relationship to the stories you lived by and you gave that to your daughters, who gave that to my mother and her sisters, and they have given it to all of us, children, grandchildren, cousins, and second cousins, all of us. The stories of the Métis Nation are the core of its identity.

Can I quote her to you, Pépé? That won't be too tiresome of me, will it? "Although other Indigenous peoples and other Canadians live on the same land and share the same state, none of these 'others' share the Métis Nation's social boundaries—its culture, social and political histories, kinship ties and cultural geography," Teillet wrote.

Still, there are times when the aunties bring out other stories, the ones not always told to everyone. I wonder, Pépé, how you would tell your own part in this story?

Seems like the world's on fire. Like the world's burning itself up.

I read an article in an online science magazine that tells about the day in 2013 when scientist Kira Hoffman spotted something unusual—sort of a grammatical inconsistency—in the rainforest in BC. She noticed an old fire-scarred western red cedar in a place fires weren't supposed to burn.

Fire isn't supposed to be part of the forests in some places. So much rain falls on the West Coast that fires are supposed to play only a minor ecological role in some regions.

But there was that fire-scarred tree Kira Hoffman saw in the hyper-maritime zone on Hecate Island, named after the Greek goddess of magic. That tree haunted her, she told the magazine writer who called to talk about her research for an article. It told a story that wasn't straight.

When did this fire burn? Kira Hoffman asked that question, and she changed the focus of her studies from soil ecology to fire ecology.

If you could list what makes someone look
Métis, whatever is on that list,
Lilian had it most, that's what
my mother's cousin told me. The aunties

remember in stories years later that Lilian looked
the most Métis of the sisters and the aunties.
She's Bob's niece and she was there
to help with the seven children.

They say Lilian wasn't sure
she wanted to claim all her relations
the one speaking from her skin and
her eyes and her cheekbones.

Back in the 1950s, she's there because
Estelle, my grandmother,
the family beauty,
can't get out of bed anymore,
depression.

She had the kind of brown eyes that could
stop a man in his tracks, they say.

Was this beauty a comfort to her then? She's
falling and falling and she can't get out of bed.

So nobody's there to stop Aunt Lilian
from setting the fire out back of the house.

Devil's Reel tune your fiddle

to A E A C# if it's an open tune you want
you've got to still the jig of the feet on the floor
if you want to play *The Devil's Dream*
The people tell stories of possession
La Double Gigue
The Devil's Breakdown
Le Reel du Pendu
In some places when the devil hears his own
songs
he accepts the invitation
takes you as his dance partner

FROM the correspondence of a Montreal paper we take the following remarks regarding Manitoba : " If farmers and agriculturalists could only be persuaded of the prospects and chances offered by this Province, they would not be afraid to risk their fortunes in it. Now is the time to come. Now the Half-breed land scrips and homesteads are being literally given away. A man can get a farm of 160 acres in many cases for $50. The finest land in the world; no manuring, no cultivation required ; just plough up and put in the crops, and the return is forty to sixty bushels to the acre. The prospects of the country were never better."

My dear Pépé,

You hold the answers to all my questions, Pépé. You are in the afterlife with the ancestors, after all. You know, I think all the stories that have been told and all the stories that will be told. The only way to begin is the traditional way, by speaking of some of our relations.

You are one of fourteen children. Born before you are Emma, May, Olive, Guillimine (sometimes spelled as Guillillemine), Annie Lucie, and Julienne. You are the first son born to your parents. After you are Josephine, Anne, Alfred, and Elzéar. You've probably noticed that's only eleven. I don't have the remaining three names with me here, though they're right there on your tongue, I know.

Our family tree says you were born in 1890 in Lorette, Manitoba, a community located about 25 kilometres southeast of Winnipeg. I find out from other sources that Lorette was settled by Métis farmers, buffalo hunters, and traders. Lorette's original name was Petite Pointe du Chênes, I imagine a cluster of little oak trees, I can see Red River carts in the yards. Most of them aren't being used for hunting anymore. Buffalo are scarce now. Instead, the carts that are still active are carrying heavy loads of goods south to Minnesota.

Your parents were both Métis, from different lineages.

Your father Maxime Goulet served as a Member of the Legislative Assembly of Manitoba and became the Minister of Agriculture for a time. He left the government before you were born. Just a year before you were born, he travelled to Paris to take part in the Wild West Show at the World Fair with four other Red River Métis. To Paris they brought two Red River carts, two trains of dogs, and a buffalo gun. They built a log house at the fair with Buffalo Bill Cody.

Your mother, Elise Genthon, was from another well-known Métis family. The famous fiddler Frédéric Genthon was your mother's brother. He stood over six feet four inches, they say. I wonder if he loomed as large in your life. Did you learn to play by listening to your uncle?

The Indigenous Peoples Atlas of Canada states, "In 1940, Métis fiddler Frédéric Genthon made the first recording of the 'Red River Jig' for posterity." But that's not entirely true, is it, Pépé?

WATCH THIS SPACE FOR
ANNOUNCEMENT

MONSTER INTER-RAILROAD

Whist — Dance

Saturday, May 12

ROYAL ALEXANDRA HOTEL

BOB GOULET'S CKY OLD-TIME ORCH.

Also

Victor and Gaiety Entertainers Orchestras.

CANADIAN PACIFIC RAILWAY
SOCIAL CLUB

TWO

A great-grandfather can be the fiddle
that sets the notes to a
life. Gets everyone's feet
dancing in the way they're meant to.
On planks or dust floors,
it doesn't matter,
just move to the rhythm of his bow,
if it's in your blood and
if you're able.

No way I put him down when
I was paying for milk
or bread
and forgot to pick him up again,
like a bank card,
a wallet,
or a receipt I didn't want
anyway.

Still, when I looked
in the usual places,

in my thumbprint
and in the layers of my own skin,
it seemed to me there was an absence.

Only traces left
in the stories told by
my mother and her older cousin.

I wasn't the only one looking for Bob Goulet,
was I? Music historians
and ethnomusicologists
found an old trail in Winnipeg,
in stories told by Manitoba Métis fiddler
Andy Dejarlis, but
they couldn't connect it to my
great-grandfather, the one
who moved to Mission.

Like the title given to the travelling
exhibit about the Métis, he was
Hiding in Plain Sight.

It's the 1950s when Lilian
comes to the house in Mission
and sets a fire.

The first time Lilian left Manitoba
was with her uncle, the Goulet fiddler.
That first time was soon after 1937, wasn't it?
Says so in his obituary.
Says about this time he moved to BC
with his daughters, Estelle and Olive,
and his wife Rose.

They were leaving the Red River Echoes behind
leaving that name to dry in the Manitoba summer
       heat.
They weren't going to perform together anymore.
They weren't going to keep up the radio show.
In 2018, his granddaughter tells me
it wasn't as easy as all that
to leave your music behind.

Lilian she's there
to help with the seven children.

On the plains when you watch for a fire, watch what the animals are doing, monitor the wind. You have to look at the earth you're living on. Learn how to notice what's growing and what's been burned before. Learn to anticipate how it might respond to heat and to flames. Build that information into your response plans. You read the history of the land you're walking on and ask about the last burning. When did fire last eat/feed this land? If it's been a long time between burns, you may get the urge to run. But you know you can only outrun the little fires and only for so long. When the large fires come, they chase you wherever you go and they eat/feed everything. The signs will be there. I see them everywhere. Mother, brothers, aunts and uncles, sisters on the run all the time. We're living through the years when fire suppression policies finally catch up with everyone.

Louis Goulet, my great-great-grandfather's brother, in the summer of what was probably the year 1868, was living through the final years of the Métis buffalo hunt, with a caravan of Métis families and Red River carts. Buffalo were scarce that summer. There was smoke. They watched for signs, for what they needed to know about the approaching fire:

"Prairie chickens began flying over very high, downwind and away from the fire, only to fall to the ground here and there, suffocated. The windspeed increased day by day and the fire moved faster and faster. Deer, antelope, elk, large hares, little prairie dogs, foxes, wolves, even the buffalo we hadn't seen since the day we left, came out of hiding as if by magic, all of them fleeing at full speed."

My dear Pépé,

How did you tell the story of your Métis identity, my dear Pépé? Was it for you the same way it is for me? This word describes your membership to a nation of people and it is a braid between you and relations you know only in stories; between the cousins, the uncles and the aunties who raised you and the relations you never knew in places you hadn't visited yet?

Maybe Métis for you was an entry into stories that you weren't supposed to have, not anymore, not if the Métis had gone away like the government wanted them to. This word Métis is a story between you and I, Pépé, more so than the words great-grandfather. This word is a story we are telling each other, each from our own places on the land and in time, and that word is a story that will invite the next generations into our circle.

Louis Riel's great-grandniece, Jean Teillet, wrote that he preferred the word Métis. It was a European word, but one claimed by a nation. She wrote that in her book, *The North-West Is Our Mother*, a book about our people. I've already told you her name, I know, but there must be so much going on where you are, you must be playing so many gigs up there, all day and all night, that I'm sure you're not keeping track of the books I've been reading about our history, here where I'm living, here where I'm bending over my desk every day and every night.

You don't need a lot of books where you are, do you? All your questions have been answered. That is such an alien idea to me, a person who is so often weighted with uncertainty and with doubt. To have all your questions answered, even the ones you didn't know enough to ask, what does such an existence feel like, Pépé? I imagine a lightness, as if a wing had rooted beside each scapula, into the dense site where the muscles attach. We need the books to be written, they are critical, and we also need the traditional Métis music to stay with us here to answer questions we don't even know need answering.

Your music, you would tell me if you were here, is a muscle. We all of us need it here in this living world, so please don't take it with you. Let me keep some of it here to share.

In the 1930s in Manitoba when you were performing with the Red River Echoes, the word Métis was a dirty word. Your family was so well-known that you couldn't escape the meaning of your last name, not in Manitoba. To hold the last name Goulet and to be the son of Maxime Goulet in that province and in those years was to be Métis in a way that carried you along like a fast-moving river.

"The Métis Nation has always been a people of many names," Teillet wrote in the book you don't need to read where you are. It's in the second-last chapter of the book and when I read it, it struck me how you are also a man of many names, how I am a woman of different names, too, in my own way. I have to laugh at myself, Pépé: it took me almost to the end of the book to see that. Here are a few of the names for the Métis Nation, some given by outsiders and some that we gave ourselves: Bois-Brûlés, Michif, Âpihtawikosisán, Métis, the flower beadwork people, Freemen, gens libres, half-breed, and Otipêyimisowak.

Fire leaves its story in the earth, though sometimes what's left behind after a fire will look crooked. If you can work out the details of a fire's relationship with a given place, you can read the stories. Fire creates so much of the world—that's my interpretation of Kira Hoffman's aching and beautiful work on fire ecology. Seems like the world's on fire, like the world's burning itself up.

1934 Winnipeg Free Press

FIDDLE AND DANCE STEP CONTESTS HELD AT MORRIS

(Special Despatch to the Free Press)

Morris, Man., Sept. 15—The largest crowd ever assembled in a building in Morris gathered on Wednesday evening to see the old time fiddling and step dancing contest. About 500 were present from Carman and St. Pierre to Emerson. Of 19 entrants to the fiddling contests the winners were: R. MacDougall, Winnipeg, 1; E.A. Parker, Carman, 2; and B. Pritchard, Winnipeg, 3. The special prize for the oldest fiddler, F. Genthon of St. Jean Baptiste, and the prize for the youngest fiddler went to **Miss Olive Goulet**, Winnipeg.

Olive and Estelle Goulet, aged 8 and 10 years, in costume of 70 years ago, did **the Red River jig** and had to respond to two encores. H. Villeneuve, Morris, J. Goeselin, St. Vincent, Minn., **E. Goulet**, Carman, A. Paradis, St. Pierre, also gave exhibitions of step dancing.

My dear Pépé,

The names you went by, Pépé, and the stories that would unravel if you could tell me about each Bob and Robert and Leon. To your daughters and your grandchildren you were Pépé, and that's how I knew you, long before I knew your first name was Bob. Were there other names, Pépé? Those who knew you as a lover, a brother, a son, or a friend must have called you other names, didn't they? The fiddlers you learned from, the fiddlers you played with, and the fiddlers who learned from you in the Métis kitchens, where soup and drink were passed around by the hands of mothers and sisters and lovers to keep the music coming on and to keep all the feet dancing together on the floor deep into the night and right into the next morning. You were one of the greats—I heard that from an interview with one of the last of the old-generation Métis fiddlers. When he was a boy trying to figure out how to hold a bow, you were in your prime, you could dance and fiddle and tell a story. Who were you those nights and what did they call you?

On the records you recorded with a studio in the 1930s you waver between Léon-Robert Goulet, Bob Goulet, and Leon Robert Goulet.

I wonder if this means you felt caught between who you wanted to be and who you had to be in order to have people listen to your music. It's only guesses I play with now. Even if I asked you and you could tell me from where you are, I don't believe you'd give it to me straight. That's not your way—or that's what all the aunties say about you.

Someone has written in ink on the label of one of the records. It's one you recorded in your house in the woods using a gramophone. The handwriting may be yours or your wife's, or one of your daughters: the name scrawled on that record is Bob Goulet. A few of the studio-recorded records bear the name Leon Robert Goulet. In the official genealogy records, in the family tree completed with an imprint from the *Société historique de Saint-Boniface*, your full name gives a different picture of at least a part of your life, doesn't it? There is heaviness or expectation in the name Léon Joseph Robert Goulet that I don't feel in the other names you were known by. But I can't know for sure if that's the way you felt when you wore that name, can I, dear Pépé?

Take a Turn, Summer 1867:

if the house
had a wood floor   if the house had
it would be creaking
steady with the rhythm
creaking   if the house
had a wood floor   if the house had
creaking with the rhythm
of dancing feet   if there was no floor
bare ground   stamping moccasins
bare ground the way it was
with the winter houses
if there was no floor   the bare ground
the way it was most places
dust rose with rhythm
bow and sash   heel and toe
dust rose and everyone
takes a turn going out
open the door   take a turn walking
out with the air
evening air   dust
have you seen it rise?

Online, I read a newspaper story out of BC that tells
of one farmer who refused to evacuate, summer of 2018.
He said it looked like lava was coming down the
mountain. He said the whole mountainside was engulfed.
He wouldn't leave and authorities said people like him
put firefighters' lives at risk. He stayed on the slight
chance that he could protect a part of his farm from what
he knew was coming, what must come, what would not
spare him, surely. He said he'd wait until it was almost
too late to evacuate. He had a plan. He'd worked out
where he'd take his herd if—no, when—a wind gust
brought the fire all the way down the mountain and
dropped it at his feet.

CASH FOR SCRIP.

Cash for Scrip.

Cash for Scrip.

I am commissioned to purchase for those concerned,

20,000 ACRES

Half-Breed Scrip.

My investments being only for others, on commission, I am free to do the best possible for those investing through me.

One Acre Lots on City Limits and one-and-a-half ch. Road,

$20 to $75 per acre.

Demands are now being made daily for Homestead, Freehold and River front farms, and several parties are now out examining locations from this office with a view to purchase. All parties having such to offer should immediately send particulars to me in time for my July list of Lots for sale. Lists issued monthly. No sale, no charge.

Farm Lots and City property for sale in all parts of the Province and city.

A few Warrants wanted immediately.

A. W. BURROWS,
opp. McKenny's Hardware Store.

a6mtf   170-189

THREE

I began looking for Bob Goulet
in my first-year college
English class.
I wrote about him and my grandmother,
the family music they played
in Winnipeg, a place I knew
nothing about.

I wrote the stories my mom
told over and over again for years,
asked questions at family gatherings.
I got good marks back then,
but where was I to go with all the stories?
where was I to carry them?
I didn't know who to ask.

> Estelle, I carried
> on my shoulders, sometimes
> like I carried my daughter
> on my shoulders,

sometimes on my back,
as a comrade in a war we didn't begin,
and sometimes, as a baby,
in my arms.
In life I hardly knew
you, mémére métisse.
I carry the hollow bones
of your dreams and walk
in the forest of your future
thick with unlit tinder and heavy
with all the fires that were suppressed,
according to government policy, the fires
passed to me, the reason I burn
everything, so bright so hard.

HALFBREED SCRIP TRANSFER FRAUDS

It didn't take much for jobs in
new cities, for student loans
and pregnancies, and a colicky baby
to displace the urgency
I'd felt over his displacement.
I lost focus, let go of the traces
until I was in my forties
and living in Newfoundland and Labrador

where I found hints of him in a Ph.D. dissertation.
Things I didn't know.
I found his name in a few lines
written by Monique Giroux,
a few lines I copied
into a funding application,
not knowing then how
connections can grow.

"Manitoba's fiddlers were first heard
on local radio stations
during the early period of radio broadcasting.
Bob (Robert Leon) Goulet was particularly well known
in the early years of Manitoba radio broadcasts,
performing with his orchestra on CKY (Winnipeg) in the
        1930s,
especially between 1933 to 1934 ("Radio Flashes" 1933).
According to Andy Dejarlis, Goulet also recorded
with RCA Victor (cited in Mackintosh 2010, 37).
Although it is not clear when Goulet began recording
(Dejarlis does not give a date),
he was likely the first fiddler in Manitoba,
and one of the first in Canada, to release an album."

She wrote "likely"

because she couldn't confirm.
The weight of Bob Goulet's name
was propped up only by old newspaper articles
and held in place by the oral histories told
by old-time fiddlers in
Manitoba, who'd played with
Bob Goulet, or only just heard of him,
Bob Goulet, the fiddler with the music that flamed
high and quick and was put out
before his talent could burn much ground.
Nobody'd heard about the Red River Echoes,
those musical Goulets who played
the traditional music for everyone,
not since they cut ties and left for
a piece of land in BC, land they could own.

"Other local fiddlers were also heard on the radio
(e.g., Jimmy Gowler "old time fiddler"
was heard on CKY in 1929) ("Radio" 1929),

although many of the fiddlers broadcast
on early twentieth-century radio in Manitoba

are now forgotten."

The tree that had been scarred by fire haunted Hoffman. It was out of place.

She had questions. When did the fire leave its mark on the red cedar? What caused the fire? How many other fires had burned in this area of temperate rainforest in British Columbia, a place where fires aren't supposed to burn?

So, Hoffman did what academics do: she studied the area.

In the end she was able to reconstruct 700 years of fire history on Hecate Island.

My dear Pépé,

Just that one word, Métis, meant our lives rushed ahead in ways that didn't always fit what we read in books and saw on television. That was the only word we used for ourselves because my father was out of our lives by the time I was five. I only ever saw my dad again a handful of times. Once, when I was fifteen, he arrived at our door without warning when mom was away for the weekend. I was in charge and the few hours we were with him were not comfortable. I've never told anyone that before, Pépé. After that, I only saw him once more before he disappeared altogether from my life.

Pépé, you held the pull of a father for me. The longing for the motherland that Teillet describes in her book became both mother and father to me. I knew what a Métis family was because I could see my grandmother, my aunties and uncles, my mother, my cousins, and my sisters and brothers. For a long time, I didn't know what a Métis Nation was. That idea so much larger than all our daily struggles for food and shelter and safety.

I'd like to know what you'd say to the definition adopted by the Métis Nation in 2002. I can almost hear how you would speak of the criteria that set out our citizenship. I can almost count how many evenings we would discuss inclusions and exclusions and culture and then just end up agreeing or disagreeing, but always with you fiddling and the rest of us dancing. It's right there on their website: "'Métis' means a person who self-identifies as Métis, is distinct from other Aboriginal peoples, is of historic Métis Nation Ancestry and who is accepted by the Métis Nation."

It's no easy task to demonstrate that you meet this criteria to become a citizen. The documentation has to be extensive and you know, Pépé, that our relations easily meet all these criteria. So many people think the Métis are just a mix of any First Nation with any non-Indigenous—and the less mixed the better. That's why there are those who misunderstand who I am because I am pale and blonde, like my older brother, traits we inherited from our red-haired father.

You were dark-eyed and dark-skinned. You could see who you were every day in Manitoba. But in British Columbia in the 1940s, the Métis Nation identity wasn't as broadly understood and your last name didn't mean Métis to anyone, so maybe sometimes you could look like something different. You spoke French and there weren't many of those in BC, so there must have been times when someone who couldn't tell the difference thought you were something else.

I don't know you well enough to really know what you'd say about the Métis Nation's definition or about Teillet's description of our people as a distinct nation. I can hear my grandmother jump in, passion and laughter kindling in her dark eyes. Teillet writes that "this means that it is not enough to have some ever-so-great Indian grandmother. One must prove, with documentary evidence, a direct ancestral connection to a member of the historic Métis Nation. Since the Métis Nation only came into existence in 1816, references to ever-so-great Indian grandmothers prior to this date and outside the geographic territory of the Métis Nation are insufficient."

You know all this of course. Why am I saying it? Just to hear myself say it, I suppose, to make up for all the times I didn't say it. You know what I mean, Pépé. Back then there weren't many people who weren't part of the nation already who wanted to claim Métis citizenship. You didn't have to prove your genealogy very often. You were a Goulet and most everyone in Manitoba knew who you belonged to.

The island I live on now
was its own country once upon.
Started as a colony, land stolen from Beothuk,
an entire People murdered so the houses could be set
          close
to the fish that were swimming in the waters off the
rock, next to the fish that could make money, next to
          houses
set upon the thin layer of soil that might offer
something green between the first full moon of June,
maybe, and the final weeks of August, best to live quick.

Fires here too,
man-made.
And old housing stock,
rows of wooden houses leaning
wall-to-wall shoulder-to-shoulder against
the wind and the sleet and whatever else.

Man I knew said he had to move out
of the old houses, buy new
in the suburbs.
All those old wooden houses,
he said, pressed up against each other,
old quarrelling lovers. One of them goes up one day
and the rest won't be able to help
themselves, they're tinder,
and the fire won't even
have to jump, it'll just
feed on all that so-called love
they hold up between them,

the old timber frames, the toxic
generations, the love, the love,
and the betrayal and the heartbreak,

He said, the old part of the city,
it'll all go up, one day,
and it made him nervous.
Matchbox houses, he said,
I couldn't risk it.

Any person having bargains to offer will do well to send me the particulars as soon as possible. I will also devote particular attention, this summer to the purchase and sale of half-breed

Scrip and Patents,

As well as the recovery of them from the assignors or land office, when issued: and undertaking the transaction of the business of making, proving, and recovering claims at the Dominion Lands Office respecting

Disputed Titles

Or homesteads, and the placing of scrip upon, or location, or purchase of Dominion lands, for settlers or speculators.

Duck Dance: a child

begins by finding a tune
                    Everyone dance forward
on the fiddle, a tune that's been there generations

                    And then dance backward
a melody heard over and over
                    Li danse de kenard

at late night fiddle sessions
                    Forward and back
older ones whispering the littler ones to sleep

                    Once, twice, more
outside the circle, by the wall
                    Trace a figure eight

don't they start with a song that's in their milk breath
                    Wind around each other
a song that lives in their fat fingers, curls into their
hum,

                    Each couple through the arch
a sound that picks up the fiddle, steals away with the
    bow
                    Dip under

takes the child by the hand
                    Then make the arch for the others
to hear what happens next

There's a digital copy
of my great-grandfather's
fiddle songs.
He is always playing,

making the "Red River Jig"
with his bow and his fiddle.
He is playing now

Which of his daughters,
the elder Olive
or grandmother Estelle
Is accompanying him on the piano
in this recording,
made in a little wooden house
in the bush in Mission.

He is always playing.
Music pours through
the cracks in the resin today,
slipping out the windows from back then,
though that house
burned down long ago—
fell for Estelle's cigarette.

There's a story auntie tells me
after I start calling, asking, knocking
at her door, sitting at her table over tea,
sharing what I can, asking
for more than I should.

She remembers a man from Vancouver
asking Pépé to play with an entire orchestra.

My mind runs on ahead,   needing
details   who   when   how
Auntie doesn't need any of that.
She grins at me, tells me
he said no, he would not

perform.

High alert: Where is the fire? Is it a risk? You can make yourself unhinged as a jealous devil watching for it, anticipating it, reacting as if even the smallest misstep has the potential to get out of control, to consume the safety you're trying to create. You pull yourself into pieces, little bits of you sent out ahead to keep the rest of you safe and what's left behind, well, it's not whole anymore is it? Alone in the city in today's world, there's only you to keep watch for the danger and the danger is everywhere, isn't it? You see the smoke; you smell the danger; where is it? And, you don't have a council like the one that led the Métis hunt caravans. The way Louis remembers it, the way the council organized to protect the group:

"The council didn't show it, but they were worried. Scouts sent out on reconnaissance were beating the flames and lighting small blazes to change the currents of air rushing to feed the main fire. They reported to the council that the fire was running along a big ridge that snaked between two muskegs."

Robert Léon Goulet taught himself
to play fiddle the way the Métis
all did back then, growing among big families
living near the Red River:
by sticking close to the other players,
getting his hands on an old fiddle
making his own sound until
it was good   and he knew it.

    He passed the fiddle
    to his daughter
    In some Métis families back then
    the fiddle was passed only to a son.
    Bob Goulet looked around
    and there was Olive
    a taut wire, electrified,
    awake to the music
    in the fiddle.

Nobody taught in a formal way.
If the music took you   you followed.

FOUR

Travel back West.
Manitoba,
Saskatchewan,
Alberta,
British Columbia,

searching for
the Red River trails,
for the echoes left
by family,
wanting to touch
my mother's stories,
hold them in hand,

like an old-time fiddler handling
a traditional Métis song.
I want to create a variation that
will be be my own.

My dear Pépé,

What did you call your grandfather? We all call you Pépé, an affectionate French word for grandfather. I don't know how it would have been back then between Métis grandfather and grandson. Which language did the relationship between the two of you speak?

Your grandfather was Jacques Goulet, one of the early Métis voyageurs. He worked first for the North West Company and then for the Hudson's Bay Company. What did you call him?

Your father would have had something to say about the title you gave to your grandfather. Articles written when your father passed away note his "mastery" of prairie First Nation languages. Like many Métis families, everyone could move between many different tongues. In which language did you address your grandfather? Did you call him by the Michif word for grandfather; did you call him moshoom? And if you did call him moshoom, would you have wanted your own grandchildren to call you by the Métis word, to call you moshoom too?

When you met your wife, she was the daughter of a well-off Québécois family. She was a young French woman set to inherit privilege and a besotted girl who gave up everything to be your wife and to birth two Métis children in Manitoba. Did she teach her grandchildren to call you Pépé to match her title, Mamé? That's the only word I ever heard you called by, unless we were explaining your music to someone who didn't know who you were. To us, you became something other than Pépé only in your music. You were always Pépé. I wonder if you ever missed the word moshoom; or did you wear this name as lightly as you wore your Roberts and Léon-Roberts and Bobs?

The forties were the Manitoba years,
the best of the music years

> Estelle was given the spoons
> the piano and the jig.
> The fiddle
> was not hers.

The fifties belonged to British Columbia.
Bob moved with his daughters, Estelle and Olive, his wife
                    Rose.
They left the Red River Echoes behind. He dissolved
the family band, left all that to Dejarlis and the others
who were coming up behind him, younger and, it could be,

not so tired   they built houses
on Canada's West Coast bought a horse to drag
the logs out of the woods. Made money from selling their
                    own trees.
Still, they had their fiddles. Olive had a piano delivered.
To the house on the land her father bought
with money made from selling old scrip rights.

Must be the 1950s. Lilian comes to the house in Mission.
My mother is little, the fifth of seven.

Faced by the prospect of fire spreading to the muskeg, Louis Goulet recalled:

"This muskeg was covered with a thick layer of humus at least a century old. It had never been burned over as long as anyone could remember. Now, dried by two years of drought, it made a veritable carpet of tinder."

Complex post-traumatic stress is a term that's come into more common use in the last decade or so. It's usually followed by the term disorder. With or without the word disorder, the term describes the long-term impacts of repeated, sustained childhood trauma that the child was never able to process or recover from. To cope, the child suppresses the events and its associated emotions, often dissociating entirely. In the short term, this saves the child from injuries, particularly where there is no community or family support. In the long term, when the child becomes an adult, there is an awful lot of unresolved debris hanging around. Some children are able to hold onto this debris just fine well into their twenties and thirties. For some of the children, it isn't until they reach a quiet point in their lives, maybe mid-life, that the debris, all that tinder, all that thirsting for spark, build up, the fire risk is severe and the time of burning begins.

FOREST BLAZES RAGE UNCHECKED

Montana and Idaho Fires Continue; Washington and Oregon Report Gains.

By the Associated Press.

SPOKANE, Wash., August 10.—Serious forest fires still burned in Montana and Idaho today, while blazes in Eastern Washington and in Oregon were reported considerably subdued.

Three conflagrations stubbornly resisted firefighters in North Idaho—the Bald Mountain, Old Man Creek and Salmon River fires. Montana foresters dispatched additional crews of men and pack trains to the fire lines in that State.

Oregon Situation Improved.

The situation in Oregon was believed better, with one fire in the Mount Rainier Forest offering the most trouble. In Western Washington only the Wolf Creek fire in the Chelan Forest seemed serious.

Although low humidity has worked against the foresters during the last few days, few new lightning fires have been reported.

More than 4,000 firefighters were trying to stem the tide of flames by cutting out underbrush, digging trenches and backfiring. Well organized bases of supplies kept them furnished with food, tools and blankets by using trucks and pack animals. The fires had burned over some 50,000 acres in the Northwest.

California Fires Under Control.

California fires were reported under control. In the northern part of the State a blaze burned over 3,000 acres of brush and pasture land near Badger, Mont. Francis Solus, firefighter, suffered a broken arm when a horse he was riding rolled over him. Cattle were destroyed and valuable pasture and oak fuel burned over. The fire started Thursday when faulty ignition set an automobile afire.

New San Luis Obispo, Calif., firefighters fought flames at the head of Lopez Canyon. The fire in Rinconada section was partially under control and the quicksilver mine was saved when the fire burned around the works. Three hundred men were on the fire lines.

SHIFT OF WIND SAVES TOWN.

Firefighters in Manitoba Get Much-Needed Relief.

WINNIPEG, Manitoba, August 10 (AP).—Forest fires, which last night swept up to a line within 300 yards of the railroad station in the little town of Rennie, Manitoba, near the Ontario border, were reported under control by forestry officials today.

The smoke-begrimed and exhausted firefighters had been driven back and were about to flee when the wind suddenly shifted and the town was saved.

Today they gained complete mastery over the fire in that area, and a part of the crew was shifted to other districts where new fires were reported. Bush fires are burning near Hector, 20 miles south of Rennie, but there is no valuable timber in that district.

The situation generally in Manitoba was much improved today, but rain was needed in many sections.

D. C. Man Is Hurt in Berlin.

BERLIN, August 11 (Sunday) (AP).—Lawrence Hoover of Washington, D. C., who is attending the advertising congress here, received slight injuries to his head in an automobile accident in which two other persons were killed. He was able to go to his hotel after first aid treatment at a West End hotel.

Friends of Charles E. Hoover, a commercial artist, with studios in The Star Building, expressed the opinion last night that the Lawrence Hoover, reported hurt in Berlin, was he. Hoover and his wife, Rochen Hoover, also an artist, are known to be in Berlin.

Parts of the Needle, Manitoba, Canada 1870:
The eye

carries the thread and the point penetrates the
        material,
either parting the threads or cutting a hole in the
        fabric.

The sewing machine needle, hardened,
        chrome-plated steel,
shank, shoulder, shaft, groove, scarf, eye, point.

The Red River, she threads generously across
        the land, offering
each narrow lot a fertile shoulder, a well-fed
        cheek, or a soft curve of soil.

(For sewing by hand, the first needles were made
        of bone or wood,
parting the threads.)

The shank of the needle is clamped by the
        needle-holder, the one God
or Gichi-manidoo. Where the shank tapers into
        the shoulder are narrow

strips of embroidered land, up to three kilometres
        deep, with a river frontage
of 150 to 250 metres, for water and travel. The
        needle either parts the threads

or cuts a hole in the fabric-tanned deerskin,
            moose hide, cloth traded
from the Europeans, confederation. The shaft
            drives the eye and thread

through the material, down to the bobbin. A
            bobbin is a cylindrical spindle, like
the wheels of a wooden cart, on which thread is
            wound.

On the back of the shaft is a cut called the
            groove, or provisional government.
The groove releases the thread into a loop so
            that the shuttle picks up the thread.

the scarf, also known as the Manitoba Act, provides
            room for the shuttle
to pass close by. There are different kinds of
            needles: universal, embroidery,

stretch, ballpoint, denim, wing, leather, metallic,
            quilting, serger, top stitching, twin,
Riel, Dumont. The eye of the needle carries the
            thread and the point penetrates

the material, either parting the threads or cutting a
            hole in the fabric.

A crooked tune uses asymmetrical phrase structures.
A tune is supposed to have a regular rhythm,
so that it's predictable,
so everyone else can play the same song, more or less.

Métis crooked tunes add and drop one or two beats
in random places, whenever.
Improvised on the spot.

The rhythm changes
every time
there's
no predicting.

Each player has their own
way. Pretty hard to accompany.
Old-time Métis fiddlers play crooked tunes when
they are performing solo, mostly

Music historians and ethnomusicologists were looking
for traces of this early Métis musician   for verifiable
                    evidence
about the man my mother and my mother's cousin
told all those stories about.

My mother and her cousin—the woman I call my auntie
the family elder—
tell different stories
but it's the same man they're talking about somehow
He was a different grandfather to each of them.

He figured in my imagination as a fiddler and a logger
a charmer and a doting husband
a man who gave up everything for his music

a man who gave up music for his family.

In their stories he figured as the centre
of the family even as they all orbited
around the woman
he made the centre of his life
                Rose Curé—
                Mamé.

We'd sit at my mother's feet and listen
to all the stories of the world
the music in my mother's stories
would make familiar songs for us
though we'd never heard
Bob—Pépé—play
though we never learned to jig
though we never held a fiddle
This man we heard so much about
made of sound and soul
this man we'd never met
made the music of our childhood.

Hoffman said it was weird, but exciting. Science and scientists said there shouldn't have been any fires there, where it's so wet. You couldn't start a fire if you tried, everyone says. But everywhere she looked there were signs of fires. Once she got going, people would come to her, say, wait there's this fire-scarred tree here, and my grandfather said a fire was over there. She took samples of the soil so that she could read the layers. Where there were fires she found layers of charcoal. And she found a lot of charcoal where fires weren't supposed to be. And she found signs of regular smaller-scale fires wherever the forest was healthy.

Takes time for a young fiddler to

learn to live in the songs
                    Growling old

The fingers have to fly ahead of all the families   strings
            calling
the way to the grass trails that will sustain the next generation

                    Man
Drop a note here
add a phrase   crooked as you like

                    Grumbling old
It's a dance, this heel-toe between what the elders give
and the rush of spring the imperative to make it new all
            over again

                    Woman
Hold to the form told in the song's name   but keep on
            moving
Don't repeat it back the same way   don't steal   make it
your own

                    Growling Grumbling
The good ones old-timers leap between seasons playing
ahead and playing back   keeping good relations

between the strings and the bow
                    Old Man Old Woman
                    Growling old man Grumbling old woman

This story auntie, I say over the phone,
I say when I sit in her kitchen and petting her dogs,
I say when she drives me around the old homeland,
tell me more about the man who asked
Pépé to play with an orchestra—

tell me so I can see it.
I was a kid, she says, just this
high. I didn't understand, you know.
They asked him to play with them,
to get his fiddle out for *The Red River Jig*.
Think it was in Vancouver, the
orchestra there.
I ask: The Vancouver Symphony
Orchestra?
Must have been, she says.

My dear Pépé,

Your father's death was reported on the front page of the *Winnipeg Tribune* on January 18, 1932, under the headline "MAXIME GOULET, MINISTER UNDER NORQUAY, DEAD" and with the subhead, "Native of St. Boniface Had Picturesque Career in West." You won't get a fat head about it, will you? Not when I remind you that it was the secondary headline on that day. Remember that? The largest and most important headline on that day in that newspaper was "51 COWS PERISH IN DAIRY FIRE, LOSS $30,000."

Probably you didn't read the newspapers in the days after your father died. Maybe this is the first time you're hearing that cows displaced your father on the front page of a newspaper, and maybe you're with him now and you're both laughing as you give him a good ribbing.

The Winnipeg Free Press story on the day of your father's death was published with a subhead that read: "Was Member of One of Oldest and Best Known Families in Province." Maxime's obituary made the front page of other newspapers on that same Monday too, though in smaller font with a bit less prominence: the *Saskatoon Star-Phoenix*, the *Calgary Herald*, and the *Winnipeg Tribune*. The *Brandon Daily Sun* printed a small story on the inside pages.

FIVE

Here's an old photograph
in the newspaper grainy
black and white undated
Bob Goulet with a bamboo and ivory
flute held to the mouth fingers
ready to play

a song I've never heard
The story of possession
of an object that
traces the male line

A time of loss
an era of losing things
language culture connections
a bamboo and ivory flute.

The story in the newspaper
printed in 1934
289 years after the flute arrived
in Canada with the first Jacques Goulet
From French Jacques Goulet down the line
to two more Jacques, French Canadian

then to the first Métis Alexis and to
the minister of Agriculture in the Manitoba
government of 1880 to his son
my great-grandfather Robert Goulet

a flute from France
it had stopped making any sound
in 1914
the song of its connection to France
superseded by the fiddle and
the "Red River Jig."

You could bring the flute
back to working order
back to its old-world connections
by steaming it the story says

steam it and it'll sing songs in French
again maybe make some Michif songs
too who knows?

By 1947 the flute had vanished
Bob Goulet's descendants
are looking for it
so it can take its place
with the fiddle songs
they keep in the cradles of all the grandchildren

The flute vanished
almost as if the final French-Canadian connection
had walked away hardly ever spoke French anymore
and the Michif passed down the line
was the language played on the fiddles

tunes that played in my dreams
filled the moon and
hung the constellations in my mother's stories

Mama never mentioned the flute
I heard about that later
For her it was the piano
and the fiddle
There was no French
in my mother's stories
just the jigging
the land
the fiddles.

This music from the prairie burns
into the hyper-maritime zone
I've created for myself here
in Newfoundland and Labrador   There is
a field along the river
where I walk
some months
it's purple with fireweed

I think about the orchestra story a lot
after auntie tells it and I wonder

if I should add it to this book,
the one that is coming together
in your hands, the one
you are reading.
I don't know   I have so few details

the things I don't know seem to expand
get in the way of the story my auntie is telling.

My dear Pépé,

There are a handful of words used to describe Goulet men in these newspapers that are like codes. They call the Goulet men descendants of the voyageurs. They call them pioneers or fans of the old-time fiddling and jigging. Sometimes they call them French-Canadian. In so many of the newspaper articles about members of the Goulet family, it's the place of birth that quietly gives away the Métis status; the reporter might write that a man had been born on an allotment along the Red River. Even just the mention of the Red River would signal Métis ancestry to those who knew.

The years you were living in Manitoba, Métis wasn't the word the newspapers used to describe the members of the Goulet family. It wasn't a word used often to describe other prominent Métis families either, including your mother's family, the Genthon line.

I did find one story that used the word Métis. The Regina *Leader* ran a note about your father's participation in the Paris Exposition. Published in June of 1889, the brief reads, in its entirety: "Ambrose D. Lepine, Michael Damas, Maxime Goulet and Jules Marion, four well-known Métis, have started for the Paris exhibition. They go to show what the climate of Manitoba can do in the way of raising large men. They have taken with them a regular half-breed outfit, and will no doubt receive a cordial welcome from their cousins in France."

The *Saint Paul Globe* in Minnesota ran a brief just a few months before that one, published under the subhead "Buffalo Bill has Collected his Manitoba Exhibit." The reporter out of Winnipeg who wrote a special to the *Globe* didn't use the word Métis at all, but said only that the Buffalo Bill's Manitoba contingent—"comprising four French half-breeds" —was leaving on Monday with two Red River carts, a buffalo-skin Indian teepee, an early-model plow, dogs, and a flintlock gun used in buffalo hunting. Either the dates are mixed up or there must have been a delay, because the two briefs offer different dates for the start of the trip.

And there's the story in 1926, the *Winnipeg Tribune* announcing your father's retirement. Did you ever read the story, Pépé? They say his health was declining and he couldn't work anymore. The word half-breed appears in that story, although it's placed kind of sideways to Maxime, almost as if they didn't want to make a direct connection: "Mr. Goulet is one of the few survivors of that relatively small group of men who made Manitoba history 50 years ago, when Indian and white man were still holding council as to their mutual relations, and half-breeds made up 35 percent of the population of the province."

TO RETIRE

MAXIME GOULET

Mr. Goulet, minister of agriculture for Manitoba, 1879 to 1888, is resigning from his post as teacher at the Dog Creek Indian School and will reside in St. Boniface.

MAXIME GOULET, NOTED PIONEER, IS RETIRING

Maxime Goulet, Dog Creek, Manitoba, former minister of agriculture for Manitoba in the cabinet of Hon. John Norquay, is about to retire from the Indian school where he has taught for the last nine years and yield to the demands of health for a life of retirement. Mr. Goulet is one of the few survivors of that relatively small group of men who made Manitoba history 50 years ago, when Indian and white man were still holding council as to their mutual relations, and half-breeds made up 35 percent of the population of the province.

Born in St. Boniface, Jan. 28, 1855, Mr. Goulet was elected to the legislature at the age of 24, defeating Hon. John Taylor in La Verendrye. He succeeded to the portfolio of agriculture formerly held by Mr. Taylor and had this ministerial office until 1888 when the Norquay administration suffered signal defeat at the hands of the Liberals under Hon. Thomas Greenway.

Since that time, Mr. Goulet has worked among the Indians of the reserves and has taken part in councils of historic significance more than once. For the past nine years, Mr. Goulet has taught in the Indian school at Dog Creek, thus concluding a life of activity among the people of that race.

On his retirement, Mr. Goulet will reside in St. Boniface.

Some say the Métis

live between
two worlds

life lived like a suspension bridge
rattling in the wind
reaching for one side and for the other

That doesn't describe what I know
about my great-grandfather
or my grandmother
my mother myself

That's the story about Métis
that was convenient

for stealing the land

Sometimes a child's traumas include debris passed along from the previous generation. Say a child's grandmother, like Estelle Goulet and her sister Olive, went to Catholic residential school, even just for a few years. Say they left the site of their homeland with their father, who couldn't stand to watch it being stolen, scrip by scrip, because they knew the promise of land rights would never be honoured. Say they left to get away from racism and mistreatment of the Métis people, but found they couldn't get away from what they were, not really, and that they couldn't burn. Say that those wounded children became wounded parents, and so on.

"A fire on the edge of the muskeg was a grave danger to the caravan for more than one reason. It was not easy to get across the muskeg, which was a three-day march in width and even more than that in length. To go around it meant a detour that would take too long this late in the year. So we'd decided to cut across, because we had no choice."

On Hecate Island Kira Hoffman unravelled a story about fire that had almost been lost. She uncovered traces of at least 16 fires that had burned between 1376 and 1893. A fire burned at a rate of once every 40 years, a density and frequency much higher than the recorded history of lightning strikes in the areas showing traces of fire.

It turns out that fire and humans have always had a lot to do with each other. Fires clustered around signs of habitation, Hoffman said. Most of the fires burned within range of one of the former villages in the study area.

"I feel that the fires were intentional. A majority of the fires, based on the patterns of the flora, would suggest that they knew exactly what they were doing."

[BY OUR OWN REPORTER.]

OTTAWA, May 5.—Sir John read a tele-gram from Mr. Street, denying that the half-breeds sold their scrip to buy rifles and ammunition, intending to join Riel.

Beadwork: pull a black thread through the Supreme Court's
decision in Daniels v. Canada
black for the dark period

tacking it close so all the pieces are tight
usually work about four beads on a row

confirming that "Indians" under section
91(24) of the Constitution Act, 1867
refers to all Aboriginal peoples
including non-status Indians and Métis

now bring the ruling back up
between the red beads on the back end
attach it to the white beads
to form the curve of one petal

secure every second bead this way
until the blood shed for land and rights
is absorbed by the soil
secure this many yellow beads
and green beads for the next

generation because historically
neither the federal nor provincial governments
acknowledged constitutional responsibility
for non-status Indians and Métis

the 2016 decision means the federal
government will enter negotiations
these beads are tight now, they will not move

go up and slide the needle through
the last bead and add more
preferably four in a traditional cultural design

the Constitution Act, 1867, states that
the federal government
has power over "Indians, and Lands
reserved for the Indians"

it can be difficult to get the thread through the beads
        the Court advised that determining who is
Métis under section 91(24)

remains a fact-driven question
to be decided on a case-by-case basis
in the future
make sure the thread stays
where you want it
where you put your fingers

four more beads and this
is going to be a blue bud
we're going to make a circle
secure it keep it from moving around

keep it tight that's the secret
keep the beads very tight
sometimes it's hard to negotiate
the thread through the beads
then you try at the other end

pick up four pink
make sure to keep them tight
to the flower some people like to make
a pattern and others just keep going

creating the design as they go these are our prairie roses

HERE AND THERE WITH
THE CAMERA

By C.P. Dettloff
(Tribune Staff Photographer)

In 1645, 289 years ago, the flute shown here arrived in Canada among the personal belongings of Jacques Goulet. It has been in the possession of the same family ever since. Today it is a treasured possession of Robert Goulet, 387 Broadway, great-great-great-grandson of the original Goulet.

At the time this bamboo and ivory flute arrived, the pilgrim Fathers were just getting used to the new country after landing at Plymouth Rock, the American war of Independence was still 130 years away and the Thirty Years' war was being fought by France and England. At this time also the "Company of New France" was formed and was granted the whole of the St. Lawrence valley. In return for a complete trade monopoly the company agreed to take to New France 300 colonists a year and it was with one of these groups that Jacques Goulet arrived.

The flute descended in the following order: Jacques Goulet (1), Jacques Goulet (2), who lived in the district of Trois Rivieres; Jacques Goulet (3), same district; Alexis Goulet, father of eight children who, with one exception, are buried in St. Boniface; Maxime Goulet, minister of agriculture in the Manitoba government of 1880; Robert Goulet, recording artist, who has recorded the "Red River Jig," which was recognized by "The Old Timers' Association" as the original. While the flute suddenly refused to emit sound some 20 years ago, it could be brought back to working order by steaming it.

Play a tune so it belongs
to you and to the song at once
just like it's lost and following

new ways and old   let it get lost   then follow it
let it go   play your tune just a little
outside the other   let it
get lost   follow the old tune and put yours

alongside it   play it like it's lost
and the next time play on the side
of the song and higher

don't repeat   are you lost?
let it get lost   send it
in a different direction
every time   play it like it's lost.

Anson Weeks Orchestra (WGN).

Oscar and Elmer (WLS).

Ferde Grofe Orchestra (CBS-WOWO, WCCO, WHAS, KSL, KMOX).

10.00 p.m.

Indian Serenader Melody Minstrel, King Solomon (CJRC) until 11.

Red River Echoes; Bob Goulet (CKY).

National Barn Dance (WLS).

Orville Knapp Orchestra (CBS-KMOX, KSL, WBBM, WHAS, WNAX, WCCO).

Jack Denny Orchestra (NBC-WJR, KOIL, KSTP, WHAM).

Paul Whiteman Orchestra; continued (NBC-WLW, WTAM, KFYR, WMAQ, KOA, WOW, WDAF).

10.15 p.m.

Ken Albrecht Orchestra (KMOX).

Ted Weems Orchestra (WGN).

SIX

Stories are harder to lose
than a flute   they can hang
about us   in our skin
genetic memory
DNA, the way we
reach backward and forward
just so we can stand here
on this land still.

And isn't a man just a story?
The Bob Goulet I was
raised with is an idea
and not just one,
but a braiding river of stories
the streams of his many selves
splitting apart and coming together
across his homeland and moving away.

Which stories would he
have me tell?

And what is the story
I am making beside his
alongside his music
as if I too am lost?

My dear Pépé,

These days I've been thinking that I'd like to spend time with your father, Pépé. I'd like to hear what he would choose to teach. Are you there with him now? What would you say if you could tell me how he has changed after living with the ancestors for so many decades? He must be like a new man, travelling the spirit world in freedom.

Down here in his lifetime, he was well-educated. Your father, Maxime, was the third son of Alexis Goulet who was one of a group of buffalo hunters who had organized to demand Métis rights to hunt and trade fairly. Your grandfather died at a time when ruling agents and companies were trying to find ways to control the Métis right to hunt and trade freely. Now that I'm looking closely, Pépé, I see all three of Alexis's sons were men whose work for Métis rights would be remembered.

Born in St. Boniface in 1855, Maxime went to college there before spending five years in the service of the Hudson's Bay Company. When he was eighteen he married Elise Genthon. When he was only 24 years old he was elected to the Manitoba legislature, and just a few years later became the Minister of Agriculture. After he retired from political life, just a few years before you were born, he turned to teaching.

Your father lived most of his adult life near a desk. Did he bring memories of buffalo hunting with his father into the legislature and the classroom? I wonder how well he played fiddle and how often he was jigging late into the night after locking his office door. Oh, Pépé, what would you tell me about this man?

Maxime's short biography in the *Winnipeg Tribune* called him a "brilliant member of the early classical courses and besides his academic duties he mastered the dialects of the prairie Indian tribes and at the same time took a prominent interest in political affairs. Part of his varied and adventurous experiences included an apprenticeship with the famous Buffalo Bill's Wild West Show."

It isn't always easy to be the son of a remarkable man, I know that, Pépé. But it sure wasn't easy to be the son of an unknown Métis man either—and you knew that too, didn't you?

For sure you'd say to me to get off my seat and move my feet to the play of the fiddle and quit thinking so much, that it's not good for me at all and you'd be right. Still, I don't think it was easy to be the son of any man in those years.

Aunt Lilian has survived fires.
In Winnipeg her brown skin
her features and her brother's music
say more than she wants to tell.

In BC with her Bible in hand
sometimes she can pass for something else,
some other bloodline   with another heritage
bearing another set of memories.

Lilian is behind the house in Mission.

When a child's ancestral history includes certain kinds of events, some people use the term intergenerational trauma. It isn't uncommon for these children to be adults when the material they are carrying around starts smouldering. These colonial-based emotional fires are suppressed and passed down until the conditions are perfect for an incredible, awe-inspiring inferno. By this time, there's no way around it. You can only go through.

Muskegs were once-marshy lowlands that had been drained by a few successive dry years and were now covered with foin à coverture, high marsh grasses made even thicker by a vigorous growth of reeds and bulrushes.... The council knew better than anybody how dangerous it would be for the caravan if the fire should move into the muskeg.

Some stories are journeys
loving the soil of the next place—
leaf and root growing
with what is there, creating
the world by sharing bloodlines,
marriage and children beginning
then following the river,
this much we share, no less
and no more.

Other stories are beadwork flowers
women's hands using colour
to tell the people how
the buffalo and snakeroot
created the Prairies for
the people who followed

and how the Red River Cart
carried the Métis to themselves
told their stories
from one end of the grasslands
to another.

Other stories are still growing
from the rhizome
waiting in the dark
some stories are still travelling,
burrs in the thick fur of bison
the ones returning to the land
that is dying without them
the burrs will come loose
when the bison love the prairie
enough to wallow again and

There are stories that travel in songs
offered up by the people. Some of our
stories are songs with the birds
that fly the length of the prairie,
the birds who look for unturned earth
long wild grasses that haven't seen a plough
the birds who know what to do when the fire comes
what to do after.
How the songs were changing then—
        scholars say Métis women's songs
        often told stories about birds
        while the songs belonging to
        First Nations women back then,
        they didn't sing about birds
        near as often—

yes, and how the songs we need to sing
are changing now.

The orchestra story is a fly on a hook
and I swallow it whole and go down
to Seymour street when I am
in Vancouver to see my cousin
and my auntie.

I visit the archives. I talk to a researcher
who is interested but busy. I search through
piles of books filled with concert listings and
brochures from the 1930s to the 1960s.
I find nothing.

That night, I search the internet, using
terms I found in the archives. I find seven
pages, a long list of Toronto Symphony Orchestra
recording history, from 1942
until 2016.

On the first page I find
a listing for *Red River Jig*,
a performance recorded in 1950,
conducted by Arthur Benjamin
RCI No. 1918.

I send the list to the VSO researcher.
Do you know what this is, I ask?
Maybe he was the man who
came to Pépé?

After I leave the archives the next day,
the researcher replies to my email and
then I have links to a short biography
Arthur Benjamin.
He was from Australia

and came to Canada, spending six years
in Vancouver, the same years Pépé was
there, the same years my auntie tells.
He created a concert series in
Vancouver that collaborated with
musicians of different cultural backgrounds.

And I have links to an audio clip
of *The Red River Jig*, conducted by
Arthur Benjamin as part of The New Concert Orchestra.
Did Pépé collaborate
with Arthur?

The destruction that comes with fire can be healthy. It can create diversity in the tree community. You can see this pyrodiversity in the northern circumpolar boreal forest. Until recently, it was assumed that pyrodiversity didn't play a major role in the history of the Coastal Temperate Rainforests of the kind found on Hecate Island and on parts of the mainland, including Mission and Ruskin.

It's a community that we take for granted until we've harvested the forest and realize we can't grow it back the way it was, though we're not entirely sure why. The community of trees emerged from the ashes of fires occurring on the landscape over a long period of time, fires with a variation of frequency, intensity, severity, size, shape and season of burn. This creates compositional range of the boreal forest, that moves between pure deciduous and mixed deciduous-coniferous to pure coniferous stands. This pattern of fires includes human-made fires and is built on a relationship with Indigenous peoples over thousands of years. It's a relationship that's been disturbed by the long reach of colonialism. The balance is off. The pattern has changed.

Governments everywhere banned the regularly set controlled smaller fires that prevented larger out-of-control fire events, regular smaller fires that sustained the land and ensured access to food, fires the trees and plant life relied on. Fires the forest relied on, fires the community relied on.

Haste to the wedding:
That was the song
often played as at the first
dance for bride and groom

They say Rose Curé met Bob Goulet
when she left home the first time alone
 on a church trip out west
away from her home and her family in Quebec.

They say she wrote home about Bob Goulet
the Métis man who played fiddle
told them she'd fallen for him
wanted to marry him.

They say her family was so alarmed—
their daughter was not going to marry
a half-breed, a Métis—so they sent for her
brought her back to Quebec took
her home right away they say.

They say Rose Curé, she did what
her parents wanted told them what
they needed to hear   They say
she promised to obey with

bowed head and chastened
words   They say she promised
never to see him again
this man who made the music
she wanted to dance to.

Bob Goulet was the kind
of man that a jeune-fille from a monied

family, a Quebecois mademoiselle,
could not forget. So she
planned another church trip

to another western mission
They say she took the money
meant for the church and the
trip and she paid for a wedding

and became Bob Goulet's wife
They say her family cut her off
the money of course and no one
saw her no one wrote for decades
They say that Rose became the centre
of her Métis family, played halfbreed
music on a guitar beside her husband

as a member of The Red River Echoes,
housed Métis daughters in her body
birthed a new line of Métis and raised
a family in the Métis way.
They say somebody

came to see her on her deathbed
snorted at her poverty said
you got what you deserved.

I don't know what she
said back They don't say
that.

GOULET—CURE

At St. Mary's Cathedral, Tuesday, Mr. Robert Goulet, son of the Hon. Maxime Goulet and Mrs. Goulet, was united in marriage to Miss Dolores Cure, daughter of Mdme. J. Cure, of Shawinigan Falls, Quebec. Only immediate relatives were present. The out of town guests were: Mdme John, and Master Horace Burgoyne of Crystal City, Man. A wedding breakfast was served at the Royal Alexandria hotel. Mr. and Mrs. Goulet left for the east and on their return will reside in Winnipeg!

All the fiddlers in the 1930s played sessions
so they could listen to each other's
tunes so they could hear their
own music alongside another's, build
the sound of community circling
around their homes
first this house then
the next guy's house
circling around their wives
and daughters
their fathers and

sons, someone
made the tea and coffee
while they played served
wild meat for the men when they
took a break when they put their fiddles

down when they'd played their fill
whose house next and whose tea
and whose milk will be stirred into
the cups and whose table will we
gather around, whose children
will be underfoot in whose chairs
will we sit up half the night
on whose floors will our feet
dance all our tunes?

SEVEN

Growing up I always heard how
Pepé, Robert Léon Goulet,
wanted to protect his daughters
from what it meant to be Métis
in Manitoba in the 1930s.

That's why they all moved to British Columbia.

I've never known what to do
after a fire,
after the emergency is officially over,
what to do with the smoking remains,
the half-consumed door frames,
the charred earth,
after the crisis passes
and everyone goes home.
I don't know how to play fiddle.

I've always evacuated
when the flames came near,
licked at the curtains of my life,
sucked the oxygen out of my lungs.

I've never stayed to see the fireweed come up.

Decades of fire-management policies like this have left us with forests that are denser than they would be if we hadn't interfered with the natural forest ecosystem. This density provides more fuel—more dead dry matter on the forest floor, more dead decaying trunks leaning against living green trees. When a fire does break out, there's so much more to burn. The fires burn hotter, higher, and leave more devastation in their wake.

Previous to today's pattern of fire suppression, naturally occurring fires would burn more quickly, taking the underbrush and the dead trees and burning out before taking too much of the living forest. Nothing survives the kind of large, sustained, high-heat infernos that have been burning recently, in California, in British Columbia, in Australia.

It's our instinct to extinguish a fire as soon as it starts to burn. We'd like to prevent all fires, anywhere. Yet, our world evolved to work with fire.

Privacy feels safer, so first I watch quietly and I don't send out a general alarm. I sleep less. I eat less. I am not always where I am—I'm often running ahead, checking the muskeg. If necessary, I'll burn a safe zone around myself so that if a fire does get close, there's nothing around me that will ignite, there's space between me and this generational fire. I won't let anybody move across.

"Scouts were sent out with instructions from the old hands who knew the ways of the prairie .... Seeing them spurring home like that, we knew the fire was into the muskeg .... The council had been expecting this and had made some preparations. They'd made a ring around us by burning over a long, circular strip of the plain to protect our wagons and pasture."

My dear Pépé,

Your father had two older brothers. Their lives must have weighed on you in such different ways, Pépé.

Here, then, is something you know very well, something I never knew: the lightness and darkness of a father's relations; the lift of being known; and the ponderous mass of all their stories and their expectations. I feel hints of it now for the first time as I dig into your stories and fall through all this black earth into another sky.

Your uncles became legends in the Métis community. They must have been something different to you, as a little boy who loved nothing more than the fiddle and complete freedom. Did they encourage your skill with the bow, Pépé? Did they invite you to sing and dance and drink or gulp tea with them late into the evenings? Did you feel you belonged?

Maybe they were boisterous uncles who wrestled with you and made you feel like a man? Or was it another way: Were they mostly absent, caught up in the work of fighting for Métis rights to schooling, to language, to land? Maybe they didn't have a lot of time to give to you, Pépé, the oldest son of Maxime Goulet.

I'm in Winnipeg when I'm invited to the apartment
of old-time Métis fiddler, one of the last
alive.

I've talked with his wife on the phone.
He can't hold the weight of the fiddle anymore,
but he plays the banjo as it rests in his lap.
He'd like a visitor, she says.

I've come to ask him if he knows anything
about my grandfather. I've come looking
for traces and echoes.

She shows me a picture of her husband,
a teen on a horse, dressed up and sitting tall.
That's when I knew I'd marry him,
she says. She was twelve at the time.

She tells stories of marriage.
She watched him quietly and
shyly for years, until he noticed
her at a dance. They were married
when she was sixteen.

He was a fiddler. One of the
best musicians of his generation.
He had a choice.
The fiddling life was hard.

Alcohol, late nights, women,
money spent faster than it came.
He took a job driving trucks.

He took a day job and
played music on the weekends.
Today, he sits at the small table

in a small apartment and because
he can't see very well
he waits for her.
She arranges his cutlery
She tells him there is the water glass
here is the napkin do you want more
tea?
she sets out his lunch for him,
shows him where she's put the condiments
where his bread is, plainly gently,
like it's an honour for her still,
to be the one he chose to have help him.

She talks to me she says
she'd put the kids to bed
drive him out to
his shows and stay
for the music
drive him back home
right after,

make sure the babies were okay
Got better when her oldest
girl got old enough to
take care of the younger
ones, less worry.
Sleep was scarce.

And there were the women
No use being jealous she said
the women who sat around her
husband at the tables where the performers
sat, these women who crowded
her man in between

sets while the other fiddlers
were playing

She laughed and said there
were times the other women
swore at her when she
walked to the front
leaned in close to her husband
and said it's time to go.
Now no use being jealous
of the women she said
He always came home
with me.

The old fiddler nodded.
He said he took a day job
went home with his wife
when she said it was time .
He says he didn't make it big time
But the other old-time fiddlers
the ones he played with back then—their
marriages didn't last their families
fell apart.

The old fiddler's grandson plays,
makes records,
the old and the new,
wins fiddling competitions.

I asked him about Bob Goulet:
had he heard of him?
He closes his eyes a moment
then opens them and repeats
the name.

Bob Goulet, he says slowly,
now my father used to play
with him.

My father used to talk about him.
Oh he was good, my father said.
He'd go out to hear Bob Goulet
play, you know.
My father would come back from sessions
at someone's house and he'd talk about
that Bob Goulet who could play
like the devil

He was the one
my father said he could tell a story
dance and fiddle at the same time.
That was rare then.

TONIGHT
BOB GOULET'S
OLD-TIME DANCE
NORMAN HALL
275 Sherbrook
ADMISSION 25c
Phone 35 055

Double Stringing: Métis

fiddlers, the old-timers,
say you could tell their music

by the double-stringing technique
two rows parallel strings

paddle and canoe travelling through
music that never did fit on the map

the way they like
to make those maps

but they travelled on those rivers
playing two strings at once

plucked at the bottom two strings
of the fiddle

and the other strings sounded
with the melody on accented beats

hard to tell a new tune from an old one
sometimes depended who was making it

their own   older players take new songs
add the double stringing

the uneven phrasing make it old-style
make it sound like it's been around

since the first Métis got to singing
and dancing in the teepees by the

carts in the log houses young
players can take an old tune and

straighten it out make it sound
like some shining dark-eyed singing

Métis kid with all the talent made
the song for the next session

Songs going back and forth straightened
out and made crooked dancing

from one string to the other balancing
on two strings at once least

that's what they say

My dear Pépé,

But look at what I've done, Pépé. One of your uncles died twenty years before you were born. He couldn't have roughhoused with you at all; his time was up before yours began. Instead you must have wrestled with his story and the events of his life and death. This must have burned into who you are and how you decided to live your life.

Your uncle, Elzéar Goulet, died a martyr. In 1870, he was chased into the Red River by members of a military expedition sent by Ottawa to the new province of Manitoba to terrorize the Métis population.

Stories of beatings, rape, and murder at the hands of members of this militia circulated widely. No arrests were ever made for these crimes. One day members of this militia spotted Elzéar and began a chase. Others joined in, including a band of vigilantes calling for his blood. Some said Elzéar had a gun on him, but chose not to use it. Desperate, Elzéar tried to swim across the river to St. Boniface, but he was pelted with stones by his pursuers and knocked unconscious. He drowned in the muddy currents of the river.

The Manitoba Historical Society website recounts the statement made by a witness, Joseph Tennant, who held the position of bugler with the Ontario Rifles, members of which had been part of the pursuit of Elzéar: "The frenzied mob in pursuit hurled missiles of all kinds at the hunted man and stoned him to death in the water."

Your uncle was a labourer, a mail carrier, and a hunter. He'd become a high-profile target because of his role in Riel's provisional government. In March of 1870, twenty years before you were born, Pépé, your uncle served on the court martial for Thomas Scott, who'd been accused and found guilty of treason against the provisional government in the Red River.

All Métis were targets. Many families left the area entirely after the militia arrived, travelling to Montana, Saskatchewan, Alberta, British Columbia, and the Northwest Territories. Some went buffalo hunting or relocated to their winter communities. So many left and in the decades after the out-migration of Métis from their homeland kept on.

Elzéar died at the age of 34. His wife, a 26-year-old Métis woman and their six children, moved in with Maxime's family. Maxime was fifteen then and this must have made an indelible impression on your father's life. It must have become a story that flowed into the lives of his children, and into your life, too, Pépé.

E|GHT

I think it's time to meet with
relations I've never met before
Two respected Métis elders
living on the Sunshine
Coast

When I call the wife answers and she
gets her husband on the line too
They talk together on the
phone one following the other
one agreeing with the other one
filling in for the other one
encouraging the other
I think of the emails we exchanged
their shared signature and quote:
"Long live the Métis!"

I'm staying in downtown Vancouver
the meeting was arranged that morning
I scramble to figure out a route
to make it to the skytrains and buses
to the ferry

I stand on the deck
listening to the mountains
as they rise every moment
from the sea singing
They greet me as family

as do my elders
when I arrive
we share family trees
papers written and read
ideas and plans

She tells me this:
be careful
you'll be criticized for
speaking out for
the Métis for
your people
for telling your story
The government
she begins, and I
don't record the rest

When we are walking
out of the coffee shop
with their son
she turns to me and says
I'm not born Métis my husband is
I married into to it
I gave birth to Métis children
I brought Métis babies into the world
she holds her hands over her lower
abdomen over her womb

I've read articles recently about the science
that shows how mothers
take on the genetic material of the babies,
articles with headlines like
BABIES CELLS CAN MANIPULATE
MOM'S BODY FOR DECADES

Mothers share all that blood
even their husband's genetic material
I remember reading this in *Aeon*:
> women are chimeras, with genetic material
> from both their parents and children
> *Where does that leave individual identity?*
> ... within weeks of conception, cells from
> > mother
> and foetus traffic back and forth across the placenta
> resulting in one becoming part of the other
> mothers ... carry at least three unique cell
> > populations
> in their bodies — their own, their mother's, and their
> > child's
> creating what biologists term a microchimera
> named for the Greek fire-breathing monster with
> the head of a lion, the body of a goat, and
> the tail of serpent

that's something
she says   that's not
nothing

My dear Pépé,

Your uncle Roger played the fiddle, that I know. But did your uncle Elzéar love the fiddle the way you did, Pépé? He must have played well; all the men of your line began as children, didn't they? Oh, Pépé, if you could answer my questions.

Your uncle Roger died in 1902, when you were twelve. Like your father, your uncle Roger was educated. He'd attended St. Boniface College and became a surveyor, a district judge, and a member of the Council of Assiniboia, which was, for a time, the governing body for the area you were born.

At one point, Roger was authorized by the Ottawa government to negotiate the Métis land claims with Métis leaders. At the same time your uncle Elzéar joined Riel's provisional government. According to the Manitoba Historical Society, Roger "was obliged to oppose Louis Riel's provisional government." Some say it was because of Roger's social standing that Elzéar was promoted in Riel's provisional government in the first place. Eight years after your uncle Elzéar's death, your father was elected to represent St. Vital in the new Manitoba legislature.

These stories, Pépé, how were they told to you? Were they sprinkled with bitterness or with hope? Or with something else I can't quite imagine from where I am here in Newfoundland and Labrador in the early part of the twenty-first century as a pandemic changes the daily shape of all our lives.

Monique Giroux's dissertation "Music, Power,
and Relations: Fiddling as a Meeting Place
Between Re-Settlers and Indigenous Nations in Manitoba"
I'm reading it
slowly—400 pages—
I'm reading it because she
mentions Bob Goulet's name
she remembers him
when so few other people
remember
she went looking for
Bob Goulet when
not many were looking
anymore

I asked Kira Hoffman how she knew where to look for signs of traditional controlled burn sites in a forest. "If it's healthy," she said. "Basically, any forest that's healthy and diverse, it's because of these burning practices."

Kira wants to build a fire management model that moves away from fire exclusion to one that includes controlled burning and traditional ecological knowledge in the planning. Like so many others, she believes it's important to understand ecosystems, to learn what they have to teach us about the land and the connectivity of life so that one day we can rebuild what we can't save. It's about understanding how the past has shaped present-day forests and using that knowledge to create the conditions that will grow healthy forests for the future, she said.

All the time checking. I don't have any water sources nearby, not to put out a fire like this. I walk along the river, but it's frozen over. The cold Atlantic Ocean would do, I think, if I could get past the ice and snow that clogs the beaches and harbours, and just dip myself in, quick. No fire can withstand that kind of cold. This is the bitterest winter in so many years, according to the people who keep track of such things. For my part, I'm not at all sure what I need. A pill to suppress this fire? Someone in a chair across from me to tell me how to breathe smoke? No, even if I put this fire out before it gets bigger, it'll find a way to burn. Fires want to burn. Fires have to burn. If not today, then in a few years from now, in a decade, when the debris I carry has piled even higher. Put down your burdens, the people who offer sympathy from chairs in offices would say. But I know it's time for these burdens to burn. Come spring if I can get near a lake, I'll swim and swim. I'd feel that I could keep safe from the inferno, keep it from taking my hands, prevent these fires from transforming my skin and my limbs to the mix of ooze and ash that fire leaves behind.

"There was a chain of sloughs along the bottom of an immense gulley which eventually went to join up with the Old Wives' River a few days march to the east of us. The council had made careful sounding of the depth of those sloughs. Finally, they'd practised manoeuvres to assure that the carts could be quickly and efficiently harnessed and moved in the direction of any sloughs that had water enough to protect them from the flames."

My dear Pépé,

The newspapers don't say this, Pépé, but my mother told me. And mama was told this by her own mother. You dropped out of school at grade three. And your father a politician and teacher: Pépé, how do I read these facts together? Your level of education is a detail that survived in our family's oral history, passed on from you to my grandmother and then to my mother.

You managed so much without education. In the generations that spread out after you, Pépé, there is pride in your choice not to follow in your father's trail when it comes to education. And there is joy and promise in the story that you chose music and freedom, business, and physical labour over your father's political trail.

Here I am, Pépé, your humble great-granddaughter confessing to you that I am without music, without even the inclination to take up an instrument or create songs. Here I am, too, Pépé, with certainly more education than is practical. I feel the need to apologize and I ease the sharp angles of graduate degrees with laughter. I know you aren't suspicious of me for taking this side route, because from where you are you can see what I am: forever a proud great-granddaughter who carries her travels through the academic world lightly, a woman still working out the route between academia and the next place she'll stay a while.

The reasons you left at grade three didn't make it to my mother's oral histories.

I know you won't be speaking directly to me from the other side, but can you direct my research a bit from where you are? Let certain hints weight heavily enough that I come to the right questions, to something approaching the story you'd like me to tell.

The most of the half-breeds who went to Carlton last summer joined Riel under oath. There is great sympathy among all the half-breeds for Riel in this part of the Territories."

Watch him as he warms up

you can always tell, you know,
can always tell if he's any good

Listen, the
music: if the songs
are freeform if they let
themselves wander
if they let
the songs get away

from the regular
metre if they get away
from playing the same beat every
time then

you can say, if
the beats change get blown away
by the huff and the wheedle and the charm of the strings,
then you can say they leapt out of
the fiddles of the French Métis

NINE

The family story keeper calls
and I answer.
She's turned a collection
of old scratched records
with labels bearing the names
of her parents and grandparents
into mp3s
The Red River Jig
The Buffalo Reel
Petit Reel Indien—
the music she remembers.

She says:
You know, what happened
to your grandmother is what happens
to a human being when they are stripped
of who they are
and are made to be ashamed
of being Métis.

My dear Pépé,

All the leavings. In the years just before and in the years after you leave Manitoba, the newspapers are littered with notices of members of Métis families leaving the area. Another Roger Goulet—a cousin, surely—left in 1939. You left the year after. I can see you playing your fiddle and discussing plans with this Roger late into the night. Would it be worth it to stay? Was there any way an uneducated Métis man could get ahead in Winnipeg? Could anyone forget you were Métis long enough for you, your wife and your daughters to live in the freedom you all desired? This Roger Goulet left St. Boniface for California, to live with his daughter who had travelled there some years before. He travelled to her and to his grandchildren. You left for British Columbia, where you knew no one.

Tʜᴇ half-breed scrip been received at the

Here it comes. Generational trauma. Flashback follows on flashback. An emotional landscape picked up by a weather event. Natural or man-made, I don't know. Feelings blown in from somewhere else, from another time, and what I feel doesn't match my self, my body, my house, my city. A personal reckoning. Stay with the suffering, the Buddhists say. I have no choice.

"As if blown by a hurricane, the fire came so quickly that herds of antelope and deer trying to escape were caught and roasted on their feet.... It is beyond the powers of the imagination to conceive of the terror that can grip one's soul at the sight of a roaring wall of flames nearly a hundred feet high."

for· St. Andrew's has Land Office.

Driving toward Waldheim, Saskatchewan

to sleep in a room
in a house I've never been to
I'm on my way to Batoche

Rented a car back there in
Saskatoon when I showed them
my credit card they told me

fifteen tornadoes since spring
Driving those roads sky darkening
I think fifteen tornadoes and I am the next

my plane touched down on asphalt, in the
approach of prairie thunderstorm
They told me

insurance will cover the damage
here's how to plug in your phone
drive straight along the rural route

fifteen tornadoes in the area since spring
and I am the sixteenth. circling the stories
the eye of the storm is in Batoche

I find my way to the work of other fire scholars. In *Awful Splendour*, Stephen J. Pyne writes that Indigenous communities "burned to shield themselves from nature's threats and randomness, to derive the benefits of fire, on their own terms ... rather than accept lightning's lottery. They sought to replace fires of chance with fires of choice."

Fire's story is crooked. Kira Hoffman dug up 700 years of fire history buried in the soil and found evidence of Indigenous people managing the forest, controlled burning practices that supported the production of food. Without these fires, the ecosystem would read differently. So much of the knowledge has been lost, Hoffman said. Although there are still elders who remember the burning of hills and mountainsides, they didn't learn how to do it.

Other research suggests that the practice dates back at least 8,500 years. Without fire, forests hang on to a lot of unnecessary debris. Stuff that can ignite unpredictably when lightning strikes or when a spark leaps from a car while changing a flat tire along the highway. In 2019, news sources reported that Indigenous cultural burning is being reintroduced in parts of Canada and the United States for the first time in almost 200 years. It's happening in other parts of the world too. Controlled fires, regular and planned, can prevent large-scale forest destruction and promote emotional healing.

My dear Pépé,

There are hints of beginnings after your father's death. The year Maxime died you were 42 years old and living in Rennie, Manitoba, hardly any distance at all from your birthplace in Lorette.

I'm sorry, Pépé, if this letter seems like a list of facts you already know, but I didn't know them, they're new to me. I'm trying to figure out what they mean to me now and what they meant back then to you.

Your father's obituary says that at his death in 1932, he was survived by his wife, five daughters and three sons, including you. You are listed as Robert Goulet, from Rennie. This is the first mention I've found in the newspapers of you, as Robert Goulet of Rennie, son of Maxime.

Your sisters included Olive, Guillimine, Emma, May, and Anne. By this time, your married sisters were beginning to move your family away from the home-land. Four of your married sisters were listed by their husbands' names and living in Winnipeg; Calgary; and Smooth Rock Falls, Ontario. Your unmarried sister, Josephine, was the last of your generation still living at home when your father died.

Your brothers were Alfred and Elzéar. You and your brothers were not living at home, but none of you had travelled any real distance. The brother named after your martyred uncle Elzéar was living in Carman, in the Pembina Valley. Fred was living in Winnipeg.

Eleven months later, in November of that year, you are Bob Goulet for the first time that I can find. I see that name in a notice advertising a gig of yours at the Normal Hall. You are not only Bob, you are Victor Artist Bob Goulet and His Orchestra. That was quite a distance to leap that year, wasn't it, Pépé?

In July of the next year, your mother, Elise, passes on. A short article appears in the *Winnipeg Tribune* about her death. The article mistakenly says she was pre-deceased by her husband, Maxime Goulet, by nearly 20 years. A mistake: they meant to print 20 months.

But I doubt you read that article or noticed the error. You were mourning. Still, your music kept you going.

From the November of the year your father died to the time you leave Manitoba altogether, your name appears almost always as Bob. The name Robert appears in a story or brief written by a reporter. In every notice or advertisement you have paid for or submitted yourself, you are Bob Goulet. There's only one more time that the name Léon will appear in the newspapers in reference to you: after you die at age fifty-two. As you exit the stage, British Columbia newspapers print obituaries that name you Leon Robert Goulet.

There are traces
in Winnipeg, Manitoba,
in the 1930s
and in Vancouver
in the 1940s and 1950s.

Notices of dances played,
advertisements for the old records
I found buried
in my auntie's closet.

Learning which ancestors to
follow, which path
to circle, which histories
to honour.

A newspaper article describes
Rennie, Manitoba, as
a railroad town
back in 1929.
Forest fires resisting
the efforts of firefighters
in Montana, Idaho, Washington
and Oregon. The headlines
in all caps:
FOREST BLAZES RAGE
UNCHECKED.

The year the land was on fire
Maxime Goulet had been retired
from politics for three years and
Bob Goulet had been married to
Rose Curé for seven years and
fires threatened everything.

On August 10,
in the Birmingham newspaper:
"Forest Fires Again Threaten Towns"
in Northern Manitoba, where
"flames again threaten the railroad town of Rennie,"
and "hundreds of men fought back the flames."

Hundreds of men. Hundreds,
and from my seat at my desk
reading these old articles
I can see all the Métis men,
the First Nations men, the
men from Europe and the men
from everywhere else,
streaked with grime
from smoke, ashes, dirt and sweat.
Bob Goulet

in the thick of it, breathing
the smoke, beating back flames,
no music, even at the day's end,
too tired to pick up a fiddle,
to breathe with the strings of the bow,
no crowds gathering,
they all pitched in to save
the town and there Bob was and
where was his Rose?
Was she with the women,

helping to feed the firefighters?
Getting ready to run,
if necessary, ready to run again?

The last sentence in that news story

tells of fires in British Columbia, where Bob Goulet
would move to in about ten years' time,
a forest fire approaching Allenby,
a fire that destroyed communication
between the towns of Princeton and Copper Mountain.
He wouldn't have taken the time to read any newspaper
                        then,
too busy doing the things men do to keep the fire away.

He must have known there were fires everywhere, though.
In ten years' time, he would leave one fire
for another, leave behind what was burning
in the prairies for what was burning
in the forests of Canada's West Coast.

In the first week of
August 1929, "the fire
that threatened to wipe
out the little town of
Rennie, Manitoba, in Canada,
was reported still serious."

Large fires were raging in Idaho, Montana, Washington and Canada, with the situation "slightly improved" in Oregon. The obstinate Bald Mountain and Old Man Creek fires in Idaho, twice reported under control, were blazing ferociously Friday night. The former covered 40 acres. The third major fire in Idaho was in the Salmon River forest, which has been ablaze 10 days.

The fire that threatened to wipe out the little town of Rennie, Manitoba, in Canada, was reported still serious.

Forest Fires Again Threaten Towns

WINNIPEG, Man., Aug. 10—(P)—Forest fires raged anew in Northern Manitoba, Saturday, where flames again threatened the railroad town of Rennie and other blazes defied foresters and volunteers.

Dry winds fanned the fires to alarming proportions and the pall of smoke spread over the country until a haze hung over this city, 80 miles from the nearest blaze.

At Rennie where hundreds of men fought back the flames Thursday, the fire again crept close to the town which appeared doomed until a shift of wind staved off the danger.

Fires were also threatening valuable timber in many districts.

In Ontario a new fire was discovered in Jacques township in the Thunder Bay district and additional men and equipment were sent into Acquest Township where a fire was raging.

A forest fire in British Columbia was approaching the mill town of Allenby and had destroyed communication between the towns of Princeton and Copper Mountina.

My dear Pépé,

Your mother's brother, was he like another father to you, Pépé, the way mine was to me? My father wasn't in my life but my uncle, he would come visit and bring us candy and gifts, tell us stories that made our sides stitch. He took us skating and stayed up late with our mother, evenings of laughter and stories of his adventures. It was like nothing else I knew.

I know now how important a mother's relations can be, her sisters and brothers. The sisters are one thing; the aunties of the world, they hold everything together. I save the details of their lives for the next telling and the next conversations. It's so much harder to find details on the lives of the women who lived in this time so the telling of their stories requires a different hand than this one does. Their stories need a place of their own, one not sidelined by the details of yours.

The thrust of your story in the time that you lived does not overlap with the lives of your sisters and your aunts as much as it does with brothers and uncles. Your uncle's and brother's lives were more directly related to yours.

From my place in history, I know how a mother's brothers, the uncles, can enter your life and expand the edges of your very self, make the edges of your body porous and open to all that is out there that you were afraid of before your uncle was there. Just by walking through the door, sharing food with your mother and your brothers and sisters at the kitchen table, just by noticing the hilarious things you do. Your mother's brother can let you know how generous and benevolent a man can be. He can show you a path in the world that is true and giving, even if you can never get enough of him and he's got to go now, no he can't stay another minute. A mother's brother can bring the whole family together, jostling to get closer to hear him tell how it was when this happened and then some. It can be this way, but sometimes it isn't.

How was it for you with your mother's brother, Frederick Genthon, Pépé? The stories Frederick would have had to tell: a fiddler so talented his music travelled over the seas, a man whose sixtieth wedding anniversary was an event that generated feature stories in newspapers from Western Canada to Montana, noting that congratulations had poured in from all over, a cablegram from the Buckingham Palace. Oh, you must have all laughed over that, talking over one another. They say he was over six foot four inches and weighed over three hundred pounds. They called him "le Gros."

He recorded a version of the "Red River Jig" in 1940, the year before he died. Did you play with him often, Pépé, over the years? Did you hold a fiddle under your chin the same way he did?

I say to my mom, maybe you've got to
have a heart that's off a bit
to play fiddle, a chest
that adds or drops the
beats your fiddle will take or leave.
Maybe you've got to have an irregular

heartbeat. I was born with an extra
beat, a murmur, was born
playing crooked in my chest, they fixed
that when I was ten

and left a scar the shape
of a bowstring up and down my chest, a trail
never traveled, not until I gave

my daughter her first fiddle
took her to lessons—learned a bit beside her.
Maybe a fiddle is a second heart

the old fiddlers held against their chests
when they played their quick rivers and their
winding tributaries, music that told how
their mamas sang to them and
spoke of the songs their papas
danced into their feet.

The fiddle, second heart
most men held
almost straight up and down,
a crooked pump
that kept their feet going
heel toe toe heel toe heel

To be in Manitoba
late in the day on August 10,
to have be ready to give it all up
to the flames, to know you've lost
the fight for your land and your home,
to give in,
and then the wind shifts and
takes the fight in another direction.
Where do the men go then?

The headline on August 11, 1929, in
a newspaper out of Washington, SHIFT OF
WIND SAVES TOWN
and "Firefighters in Manitoba
Get Much-Needed Relief."

Keeping track of the
resources on the other side
of the American border, the newspapers always
track the value of the timber threatened
or burned:
"Fires were also threatening
valuable timber
in many districts" and

"Forest Fires, which
last night swept up to a line
within 300 yards of the railroad station
in the little town of Rennie, Manitoba,
near the Ontario border,
were reported under control
by forestry officials today. The
smoke-begrimed and exhausted

firefighters had been driven back
and were about to flee when
the wind suddenly shifted and the town
was saved. Today they gained complete
mastery over the fire
in that area, and a part of the crew
was shifted to other districts
where new fires are burning near Hector,
20 miles south of Rennie, but
there is no valuable timber
in that district. The situation
generally in Manitoba was much
improved today, but rain was needed
in many sections."

TEN

Auntie is moving, so
everything is in boxes.

She tells stories,
takes my cousin and I
on a ride to see the land
she grew up on, the land
Bob bought back then.

At the end of the day
we pick through stacks of
papers, pictures, records
pulled from closets she
hasn't opened to anyone
in who can tell
how long?
What keeps coming back to me is
the feel of the records
in my hands, their unexpected
lightness

My dear Pépé,

The trail left behind in newspaper notices. In 1932 you are listed as "Bob Goulet's Old Time Dance," and your name appears in the "Dancing and Social" section of the *Winnipeg Tribune*. The listings tell me that by the spring of 1934, you are performing regularly: Bob Goulet's CKY and CJRC Old-Time Fiddler; Bob Goulet Old Time Music; Bob Goulet's CKY Old-Time Orchestra and Victor Recording Artists. You played at the parties of well-known families and you played for barn dances. You played at railroad company events and you sponsored a fiddling competition. You played at empty stocking fund events and every Friday you were the headliner at the Columbus Hall.

The summer of 1934 brings a change. For the first time there is the Red River Echoes: "Bob Goulet and his Red River Echoes" "Red River Echoes, Bob Goulet (CJRC)" "Bob Goulet's Red River Echoes." The Red River Echoes was formed when the family performed together: you, your wife, your sister, and your two daughters. By the end of 1934, the name of the band was prominent enough that sometimes it was just listed on its own, without your name: "Red River Echoes (CRC-CKY)."

WONDERLAND

BARGAIN HOUR—6-7, 20c

Grace Moore
in
ONE NIGHT OF LOVE

4 Stars
from Liberty

ON THE STAGE
BOB GOULET AND HIS
RED RIVER ECHOES

CRESCENT

ALEXANDER DUMAS

The Count of Monte Cristo

Starring: (General)
ROBERT DONAT and ELISSA LANDI
MICKEY MOUSE CARTOON—NEWS

ARLINGTON

Today—Bargain Hour, 6-7, Adults 20c
"COLLEGE RHYTHM," with Joe Penner,
Lanny Ross, Jack Oakie, Helen Mack
On the Stage at 8.15 p.m.: Bob Goulet and
His Red River Echoes   (General)

It ends quickly for some. People can emerge in a short time safe and unharmed and tell the tale that inspires audiences. For others—for me, I guess—the fire goes on and on, approaching and receding, attacking and retreating for the entire season, for years.

"When the whirlwind of fire passed over our heads it was over so quickly nobody had time to think about what had happened. In the space of less than one minute, the burst of flame engulfed us, and the next minute it was gone. Not a single person had so much as a scratch."

Reasons for traditional controlled burning:

fireproofing
ceremonies
pest management
economic extortion
clearing the land for easier travel
felling trees
as a tactic of battle
signalling
crop management: improve growth and yields
clearing riparian areas: the river breathes better
burning to help the hunting so the animals will
             come

Areas that are wildfire prone, they say, include British Columbia, California, and Tasmania. The headlines I read say so much in just a few words:

Urban sprawl and bad planning fueling future infernos.

Humans still mostly responsible for West's intensifying blazes.

What can we do?

A Note to My Relations:

It's not indifference,
this way of moving on and moving on,
it's enlightenment.
They're only encouraging us toward
a higher consciousness.
Land is the plank
in our collective eyes. Just let it go.
Remember that non-attachment
is a state in which a person overcomes
attachment to desire for things,
people or worldly concepts
(but mostly land).

We aren't indifferent, are we? We've accepted
impermanence. And we've
avoided a world of pain: Look how
they suffer under the narrow-minded
weight of owning our land.
Because we were forced to let go
we've reached the state of being
objective, of not clinging—

As you move
toward truly being one with the
universe, you'll find there are so many things
you can let go.
Your culture, for example,

and the sticky narrative that land is
our collective mother and
essential to sovereignty.
Oh, we've been allowed to let go

of that earth connection. That is
this country's gift to us.
The land claims denied,
the children taken away,
the residential schools, the mothers
and the fathers and the aunts and uncles and
grandmothers and grandfathers
forced to hide or move
or start over again, over again.

The best thing we learned
was to let go. This place we're at,
it springs from a deep consideration—
front-row seats, in real time—
of the conditions of human existence.
And we weren't going
to get to this place of
enlightenment on our own.

It wasn't until months later
after I'd shared pictures
of those records with
ethnomusicologist Monique Giroux
that I knew what I held
in my hands.

The records I'd moved around
carrying boxes holding them in
lifting them out taking pictures
these fragile things
are among the first recordings ever made
of Métis traditional music.

Giroux asks about the women in the family,
did they play?

I write back to Giroux
ask if she knows anything else
She writes officially they say there weren't many
women fiddlers, that's what they've always said.
She says, I've been talking
to fiddling families
and it seems like there's always been
women playing the fiddle,
there's always stories about them.

It's the Mount Hicks wildfire the farmer is up against. It's just north of Agassiz and it keeps on expanding in this last week of August, now 250 hectares in size. A nasty fire. Firefighters are struggling. Slopes are steep, trees are big and poorly rooted. There's a power line on both sides of the fire. He's not leaving.

"It's what we're doing
to the earth" says
our family story keeper
over the phone from BC.

I've called to ask if she's okay.
She fine, she says,
but she's been staying inside.
Says the smoke and haze from the fires
burns the sky the colour of sunset, right there
in the middle of a summer day.

She's Olive's daughter. She keeps a
fiddle in the closet
in her spare room.
Takes it out to play sometimes, still.

In some Métis families
the fiddle was passed down, not just the
instrument, but the songs and the skill
And the 'come to the session' and the 'listen
to us play'

In some Métis families
the fiddle passed
to the son most committed
to playing
the one who'd listen until
he could play the song
back to you
and you knew he
wouldn't stop if it got
hard even if you told

him to stop or you'd
give him what for.

In our family, that son
was Olive.
In our family, that son
was a daughter
who couldn't get the
music out of her hair,
born with a heart
in a fiddle and a lung
beneath the pedal of
a piano.

ELEVEN

The old records
they're brittle.
But they still offer, still play
all their songs.

I'm playing them now—
at first I wasn't any good at it,
wasn't used to the back and forth
the call and answer, and
I didn't know how to hear.

Had to sit down, didn't I,
pick my way
through all that Bob Goulet had to teach
with all the music of his life
and there it was,
the way to begin.

My dear Pépé,

On July 1, 1933, your name is announced as the new feature show in the "On the Air" radio section of the newspaper, descriptions and highlights of radio shows and listings. "Another new feature for Wednesday will be old-time tunes by Bob Goulet, old time fiddler, to be broadcast at 9.45." Your brand new show is part of the broadcaster's response to requests for more Western Canadian regional programming. How did you feel, Pépé, to have your first radio gig at 43 years old? What did great-grandma say, your Rose?

Every Wednesday for the next few years, you performed for radio audiences. Your name is listed with CRC-CKY and CJRC. In the listings, in tiny black print, you are there for the first time on July 5, 1933, Bob Goulet, Fiddler (CKY).

Oh, Pépé, the day of your second show with CKY there's another notice in the classified section, a few columns away from the radio listings. On July 12, 1933, a few lines note that your mother Elise has been buried in St. Mary's Cemetery. Did you play for your listeners that night, Pépé? The listings don't say. If you did, could the listeners hear the grief in your music?

Carry on, carry on. It's over. Carry on. What else can you do? There is something whole left beneath the soil of the burn site, just enough for another beginning, for another day's travel. The fires will come again. I will ask them to come: who can be afraid now? The next fires will be smaller. I will know how long to let them burn and how to check their consumption and change their course. I know myself now. The path that opens in their wake is the one I will walk. That is enough.

"When the crier had given the order for the wagons to drive into the water in the sloughs, it was done without a word. Once the fire had passed, the same order prevailed, in reverse. No sooner were the wagons out of the water than the oxen were unhitched in the glow of retreating flames. Not long after, the first light of dawn appeared. An hour later, the tents were pitched and everybody bedded down except for the guards."

A Primer on Non-attachment for Half-breeds: First

let go of your land. Ownership
blocks the pathway
to higher consciousness. Second

don't worry about the past or the future
let things be
All will continue the way it always

has and always will.   Third
remember life is impermanent
so are land claims. Fourth

anger blocks transcendence
and tethers you to this world
meditation can be used to numb anger. Fifth

if you do find yourself feeling anger
imagine cutting it away
with a pair of children's scissors. Sixth

there's no bliss in land, not for you.
it's a colonial thing   you don't need land
you are on your way toward god consciousness. Seventh,

be grateful for being.
You don't need that land
Learn how to forget. Memory is heavy

Anyway, how many
generations has it been?
Would you recognize your own land

if you were walking on it?

My dear Pépé,

By 1935 there are a number of Métis musicians whose notices appear alongside yours in the classifieds. The biggest name that I recognize is Andy Desjarlis. I'm interested in the variations of the spelling of Andy's in these ads. Were these mistakes, or did Andy play with the spelling of the name he wanted to use? Maybe it didn't matter at all to him at the time. The name of his band changes over the years, too, moving between Red River Mates and Red River Settlers. Andy takes the Thursday night spot at Columbus Hall, before your Friday night gigs. He occasionally appears in the radio show listings, too.

For you, Pépé, there's a pattern that emerges in 1935: you paid for classifieds saying that Bob Goulet's Orchestra is "available for engagements." The names of the people in the orchestra are not listed. These often appear above ads placed for Andy Desjarlis and His Red River Mates.

Between 1935 and 1936, you are out every weekend and many days of the week playing for people. You play on your own or you play with the orchestra or you play with the Red River Echoes. The trail ends in 1937 and shortly after you moved on to British Columbia.

Did Andy come and visit you in British Columbia? Andy's name appears in the newspapers in 1947, connected to a couple of performances near where you lived at the time. But only in that one year, at least that's all I could find. For years after that, the papers show a regular schedule of performances in Manitoba.

You talked about teaching Andy. That's what Olive's daughter recalls. She says Andy picked up a lot by playing with you. Tell me more about that, Pépé.

Andy keeps on in the music scene after you leave. Did you follow his career after you left, Pépé? By 1944 he seems to be as popular as you were in 1934, headlining as Andy Dejarlis and His Early Settlers. He becomes more popular still after that, becoming a legend in Métis music.

The last notice of you I can find in the classifieds in Manitoba is this one, a few lines appearing on Friday November 7, 1937: "Bob Goulet's Old-Time Dance. TONIGHT — COLUMBUS HALL. Admission 25c. Spot Prizes. 9 to 1."

— TONIGHT —
OLD - TIME DANCE
COLUMBUS HALL
Bob Goulet and His Red River Echoes
8.30 p.m.   Admission, 25c.

When the burn is over it will
be the time of fireweed.

The fireweed will set its roots down
right here among us all and play us a half-breed tune
on my great-grandfather's fiddle
and my grandmother's spoons.

The purple flowers on all the moccasins
will dance the rhythms, while the spoons and the bow

recreate the songs heard for generations on the prairies.

In British Columbia,
it's a person appointed under the
Emergency Program Act
who holds the power to begin
the emergency and to end it.

In Newfoundland,
a person is appointed
in the same way.

Who has that power
in Métis families?
The aunts or the uncles
the ancestors
the generations coming up?

>Must be late 1950s when Lilian comes to the house
>   in Mission,
>when they asked if she'd help with the kids.
>The fire out back of the house
>is leaping and jigging. The relation we all call
>Aunt Lilian is burning
>old papers, photos,
>anything she can get her hands on,
>anything that shows that we are Métis,
>Anything that ties the family
>to the Métis settlements in Manitoba.
>All the grandmothers and grandfathers into the fire.

There was so much
space back then and
the prairies remember
the way the tunes travelled
from one dance to the next,
from west to east and back again.

The land still holds all the versions
the players created and here
on my computer I have
a file that holds all the
scratchy digital recordings
left that remember
my great-grandfather's playing.

The trails always go both ways—
it doesn't matter which way
you choose to walk them.

TERMS STRICTLY CASH.

D. G. McBAIN.

P.S.---Scrip, Half-breed Lands, and Minor Claims taken in
exchange for goods.   D. G. McB.

My dear Pépé,

In November of 1936, there is a classified ad that I almost missed. It offers something, but I don't know what exactly, not for sure. It appears a few years before you left your music career in Manitoba. On Nov. 3, 1935, this small ad appeared: "2 FINE OLD VIOLINS WILL SACRI-fice. $15 and $20. Bob Goulet. Ph. 45 602." Whose violins were those? You kept playing in Manitoba, and so did your daughter. You kept fiddles for yourselves to take to British Columbia, didn't you? These are "fine old violins" and you were willing to take less than they were worth. So maybe this was an emergency of some sort? This was the thirties and you were a musician, and Métis. And yet, I wonder about other things that may have been going on, too. Oh, Pépé—the violins.

2 FINE OLD VIOLINS—WILL SACRI-fice, $15 and $20. Bob Goulet. Ph. 45 602.

I don't ask auntie why
Pépé said no to the man
with the orchestra.

All my questions
get in the way
and I wait for her
tell what needs
to be told.

She leans forward in her
chair and laughs out loud
the way she does.

No, he wouldn't perform
with them, she says,
but he said he'd teach them.

What? I said, gaping
like the little fish I become
when I'm listening to auntie's stories,
all gills and eating the hook.
Yeah, she says, Pépé
said he didn't need to
play for them and
how else was the music
going to be passed on
if these people who loved
violins didn't learn it too?

He went down there and he
taught them. And they paid him for it.
Not much of course, and the money

he got he gave
to his daughters.

He just wanted to pass the music on,
so he said he'd go teach
those orchestra musicians
if they wanted to learn his way
of making music. It all
made him laugh,
you know?

TWELVE

How to live with fire: the Jack pine

has cones that require
the heat of fire to release
the next generation.
These are
fire-activated
seeds.

The cones only open after a fire
has melted the resin.
There are shrubs and plants
that only sprout in smoke,
only after they sense the chemicals
that signal an approaching fire.

The European sow thistle
will invade burn sites in Saskatchewan.
In Newfoundland and Labrador
fireweed proliferates after
a fire, and it's only after
research that I learn how fireweed
will grow in parts of every province
and territory in Canada and across

Northern United States. I don't remember
seeing any fireweed growing up—could be
I didn't know how to look.

Other plants,
the Australian grass tree or South African aloes
and their cousins,
choose insulation:
thick bark or dense plant matter
that protects against damage to vital
tissues. The fire lily agrees
to flower only in ash-fertilized soil.

There are species,
relations of the pine or the Eucalyptus,
that develop a tall crown,
ridding themselves of their vulnerable
lower branches. In this way they survive flames
with only minor damage, just a little
charring on the lower trunks tells
the story of their ordeal.

These healing strategies
only work if the fire is not
a raging inferno
fuelled by decades or more
of fire suppression
policies.

In the ashes I've been sifting through,
I haven't found Bob Goulet.
I'll spend the rest of my life
looking for this man whose stories
loved me into being.

Soon I'll go looking for
his brother Elzéar Goulet—
but that's a story I'll tell another time.

These days I'm down here
in a corner in a basement, here
where the shadows of the women are put
and I think I'll sit with them
for a while, pull
at a few of the cobwebs,
frighten the spiders away.

Nights awake staring at the ceiling, knowing come morning, wind may bring the wall of fire again.

"It was a long, long time before I could get to sleep that night, even though I was exhausted. I just couldn't clear my mind of the ghastly scene that had unfolded before my frightened eyes and was there still. Terrifying howls of wolves came from here and there, as if they wanted to shout their distress to each other. They sounded like lost souls desperately trying to drown out the echoes of hell."

I walk back into my fire and look straight at my heartbreak, and my mother's, and my grand-mother's, and my great-grandfather's. I let it engulf me, let it take the grazing land. Fire is hungry and I let it feed, let it take all that underbrush, all the dried-out dreams, all the tinder pain, all of it. What will come after? Where will I go then?

"An enormous red sun was rising through the smoke-filled air when at last I lost any notion of things and men, numbed by a soothing sleep that made me forget my terrible nightmare of the evening before, the panic among the harnessed animals, the roar of the flames, hell and its howls of the damned .... Fifteen days later we were at the Judith Basin. What awaited us there was, as far as I know, the greatest disappointment in our history. Prairie fires had caused even more destruction here than in Canadian territory. Famished for grazing land, the buffalo were forced to move northward and eastward away from their normal habitat."

My dear Pépé,

They say you left Winnipeg for your daughters. You left to get them away from the racism and sexism they'd face in Manitoba. The women in the family who've kept the stories safe from fire say this, but not much more.

The women who tell our stories don't add any opinion. They don't talk to me about how it all turned out or how it might have been different.

Did something happen, Pépé?

You'd been working so hard to make your musical career work right there, where your people were from. Did something happen one day that was just too much?

I'm near the end of these letters and there's so much I don't know. I have more questions now than I've ever had.

My daughters had been home from school for weeks and there was still snow on the ground here when I first read that article about your death. It wasn't an obituary. It was a story about a man whose death was newsworthy. In those lines, I read about a man who didn't fit the shape of the stories of my mother and my aunties. Though, maybe it's carelessness on my part, a failure to listen to the stories in the proper way. In this story, you were an independent contractor of sorts in BC. Is this you, too? I look further into the records in Manitoba and I see that you ran a business there too, or tried to. Maybe you couldn't get ahead in Manitoba; you were known as a Métis man who played the old tunes on an old fiddle. All the networking and connections that come with selling and buying—maybe they just wouldn't happen in a place where everyone knows you're from an old Métis family, one connected to Riel's provisional government.

Everyone says you left Winnipeg to give your daughters a better life. From my house now, I wait for the snow to melt. I watch online updates about the number of cases of COVID-19 in the province and in the country. I watch my daughters try and fail to attend online classes regularly. My partner and I discuss whether or not our jobs are secure given what is happening in the world now. I apply for jobs in cities across the country. My partner attends endless meetings through his computer screen. And yet, there is a stillness in all of this that holds us all together more tightly than ever before. I wonder, Pépé, if there really is a better life waiting somewhere else?

My auntie sends me
mp3s, digital copies
of the records she keeps in boxes,
of the records that won't break
during the process of transformation.

I download it and I press play.

I hear cooing, first. A baby who might be my
Mom, I'm told later.

And then the piano begins.
Who's playing the piano? I have
to know. Olive or Estelle? My grandmother
or her older sister?
Maybe Olive, says my auntie. Probably
Olive.

I know who she is by listening
to her music. This is a shock, cold water
that takes me from a half-sleep. I know
her depths, her passions, her moods.

In her music I hear someone like
myself. I recognize how this woman
sees the world, how it spins and tilts beneath her
feet, how she feels sometimes she's
clinging to a merry-go-round,

how she wants to be at home
and also to be on the road.
playing the piano.
She hates anything that

holds her down,

anything that separates her from
this expression.   I know
how much time she's spent
walking with injustice,
how her music is a demand to be loved
in a world that hasn't loved
her yet, and the way she has to live
so far away from her
homeland. I recognize how she hates
the decisions she's had to make sometimes,
how much fight she has,
how she can knock a man down
without half-trying.

She'll lie down in the middle
of a freeway for the man she's chosen.
She'll walk away from the brink of falling apart,
spine straight, limbs trembling.
I know her from her music now
and not just from the stories. How
that turns everything on its head.

I listen to Bob's music too, and I am moved,
and my heart aches and tears fill my eyes, but
        I don't
know him in the same way, don't recognize him.
She was a poet who used music to make her
        poems.

I am a musician
who uses words to make songs I am
taut wire awake electrified   Who
is on the piano — Estelle or Olive?

And then Monique Giroux,
the ethnomusicologist,
sends me one page from
a score she's found.

She drops it in a text just as I'm
wrangling with the final edits
for this book and
it takes me a few days to
open it up.
Then, there he is,

Pépé appearing now in the
notes before a score from 1945
for *The Red River Jig*
"taken down from the playing of Bob
Goulet, himself a fourth generation
country-fiddler,
and to him my thanks are due."
The note is written by A.B.,
the Arthur Benjamin I've
been following to get
closer to my great-grandfather.

There's been a slight delay,
a small mistake that opens up
enough time to drop this
story in, right here.

I can't remember telling
Monique about Arthur Benjamin
or my auntie's story, but

it doesn't matter because here
it is, a place to stop for a rest.

Arthur writes, "I have heard of one family,
of mixed French and Red Indian blood,
who have been country fiddlers for generations.
Today the 'Red River Jig' is the favourite
tune of the district and no 'Old-Time' dance is complete
without it. In one of the figures, the foot
is held off the ground for a beat, and this
would account for the irregular bar-rhythms of the Jig."

In these notes found in
a vintage book shop in the UK
my great-grand-father is a "country fiddler."
And I wonder if Pépé would agree or how
he would wear that term. Did he see
this note, I wonder? I can
hear him laugh.

I text auntie to tell her about the score. Send
it to me, she texts back.
I do.

To Clare_ Christmas 1946

THE RED RIVER JIG

DURATION 2½ mins.

ARTHUR BENJAMIN

My dear Pépé,

You gave your children music. It seems to me that Estelle and Olive between them played every other instrument they ever laid hands on. Bones, spoons, organs, guitars, pianos, fiddle. Only one sister picked up the fiddle. Their music will become the soundtrack from which my mother's stories grow.

In 1934, Olive and Estelle first made their appearance in the *Winnipeg Tribune* at an event you organized. "2,000 PEOPLE ENJOY DANCES OF EARLY DAYS" the headline reads. "Bob supplied the music...the pace was fast and furious." An old married couple danced the "Red River Jig" in old Métis dress and "were followed by Olive Goulet, 11, and Estelle Goulet, 7, who executed the same steps in similar dress." There's a list of old-timers in attendance, names that reach back to the Resistance, elders you knew well. The music you played kept the memories alive. That news story ends with a description that reveals more than it means to about the way non-Métis saw you and your relations: "As the dance finally broke up regrets for the good old days were mingled with expressions of pleasure that such replicas of the parties of Winnipeg's early days could still be enjoyed by those who recalled them so vividly."

How many evenings did you spend jigging with your daughters? That same month in 1934 Olive and Estelle Goulet won third place in the "Red

2,000 PEOPLE ENJOY DANCES OF EARLY DAYS

A scene decidedly in contrast with its modern setting was presented Monday night at the Auditorium when more than 2,000 persons, pioneers of the city and district, gathered to enjoy an old-time dance. The affair was organized by Robert Goulet, whose family have been residents of the district for more than 100 years.

Bob supplied the music, assisted in a few old favorites by Bert Pritchard. The pace was fast and furious, but the enjoyment of all was so great that the only pauses occurred during the special entertainment features.

These consisted of the performance of the dances of yesterday by couples dressed in the costume of the time. Mrs. Ritchie and Mr. Jack Berard danced the Red River Jig in the costumes of 70 years ago, and were followed by Olive Goulet, 11, and Estelle Goulet, 7, who executed the same steps in similar dress.

Among the old-timers present were: Mr. James McLean, of Winnipeg; Jack McDonald, Winnipeg; John Nesbitt, Fort Garry; Mrs. Christie Bowne, Winnipeg; Mrs. Laroche, Winnipeg; Sam Smith, St. James; Alex Tate, Winnipeg; J. Gallant, Winnipeg; H. Theroux, Transcona; Ed Goulet, Carman and many more who escaped immediate identification in the crowd.

As the dance finally broke up, regrets for the good old days were mingled with expressions of pleasure that such replicas of the parties of Winnipeg's early days could still be enjoyed by those who recalled them so vividly.

River Jig" competition at the Transcona Fair. In September, "The largest crowd ever assembled in a building in Morris gathered on Wednesday evening to see the old time fiddlers and step dancing contest." Olive and Estelle again performed the "Red River Jig" and "had to respond to two encores." Miss Olive Goulet from Winnipeg was awarded the prize for the youngest fiddler.

Just a few weeks later they performed at the St. Vital Sanatorium as "Bob Goulet and his Old-time orchestra," opening their third season as performers. Also on the program "were the following; Mrs. Goulet, at the piano: Olive and Estelle Goulet, violin and 'bones' respectively; Slim Butler, guitar and yodeling, and Leslie Penwarden Mandolin and vocalist."

In 1935, the *Tribune* prints a story about a King Edward Hospital saying that "Robert Goulet, Mrs. Goulet, Misses Olive and Estelle Goulet" were part of the entertainment line-up. There's a longer trail of notices in the newspaper about parties given by notable families that list Bob and Olive Goulet as featured entertainers.

Did you worry about Olive and Estelle following you and Rose around to all these gigs? Maybe Rose worried. The stories hint that your daughters loved being at these events and near the music until late into the night. How did you all get home from these venues? Did you sleep the night out sometimes, rather than travel the roads and streets that late?

Your older daughter, Olive, chose the fiddle and Estelle did not. There is something to this choice, though I have to be careful, don't I? There's too much I don't know, too much that was never spoken.

It isn't until the year 1943 that I find your oldest daughter in the newspapers again, Pépé. She's in British Columbia at this point, with you and her sister and her mother. By 1943 your names are often given equal weight in the newspapers: "BOB AND OLIVE GOULET" and "Famous Winnipeg radio and Victor recording Artist and her Red River Echoes, every Thursday commencing Oct. 7 ...."

Her Red River Echoes now.

You did this. You passed the musical career on to her talent, her passion, and her youth. You're still a part of the Métis music scene in British Columbia. I still find listings for Bob and Olive Goulet here and there, now and then.

In 1950, when you are 60 years old—five years before you die—the *Chilliwack Progress* reports that you placed third in a fiddle contest at a crowded agricultural hall. Almost 1,500 people squeezed in to hear and see the old-time fiddling and Red River style dancing. I can find no other listings after that.

You were performing less. Taking on fewer gigs of the kind that'd make the newspaper at all. All that you were leaving to your daughter, to Olive. You were busy, weren't you, Pépé? Working damn hard, so the stories say about your time in BC. Damn hard.

Olive stepped into your shoes. If I read the newspaper articles right, the transition was happening between 1943 and 1944. You were helping her set up a solid career as a musician, weren't you, Pépé? She had become so talented a fiddler and so beautiful a pianist you felt she was ready. You were right: listening to some of those old recordings leaves me drowning in emotion. In 1943, mentions of your name in the newspapers decline. By 1944, Olive's name appears on her own. After that, she leaves a trail in the newspapers that is similar to the one you left in the Winnipeg newspaper in the 1930s. There are classifieds stating Olive Goulet and her Orchestra are open for engagement; there are advertisements inviting the public to the White Rose Ballroom where Olive Goulet will perform.

You stayed on your land up in the woods on the West Coast of the province. For a long while, the nearest neighbours were a few hours walk away and that's the way you liked it. Olive and Estelle pined for the Vancouver dance and music scene. Olive pointed her future at a music career. You helped make that happen for her.

OPENING DANCE
Old Time and Modern
White Rose Ballroom
BOB AND OLIVE GOULET
Famous Winnipeg radio and Victor recording artist, and her Red River Echoes, every Thursday commencing Oct. 7. Dancing 9-12. Everyone welcome. Service men free.

MODERN AND OLD-TIME DANCE

Every Thursday White Rose Ballroom Olive Goulet and her orchestra open for engagement. FAir. 3877.

BOB AND OLIVE GOULET'S OLD-time dance, White Rose Ballroom, every Thursday. Service men free.

OLD-TIME DANCES EVERY TUESday. Thursday and Saturday.

The devil can take hold of you while you're playing

some of the old time fiddlers say
If you start the song out the wrong way

the devil will possess your feet your shoes
your moccasins your socks will dance and

leap like a blaze you will rise up into the air
unable to stop

Some have seen this happen

Someone gets home finds Aunt Lilian
The fiddles
Where are the fiddles?
Robert's old fiddle?
The fiddle Olive played
the one given to her
when she was a child
teaching herself to hold a bow
the one that came to life
in her musical hands?
Burning.

AFTERWORD

And here's an article, found
when I thought I'd gathered everything
there was, and here, an article
in a Vancouver paper that no one
in the family has seen, one that records
the black ink of my grandmother's
big-sky self.
This old article pulled at a thread from her past and
tugged me toward her future
and my own. A photo in a newspaper,

a cutline, and so much
of that woman is there, shaking
with the effort to hold it all within
the confines of a few column inches,
a 16-year-old Métis girl running after
all that life might have to offer, and
now that I've saved it and printed it out she's
here with me in Newfoundland,
Bob Goulet's youngest daughter here

on Canada's other coast,
the girl who didn't play the fiddle, but

kept all those old mini-organs in her house,
who built the music of her life
with those instruments
until those last days
in a hospital in Calgary, that
Grandmother my grandmother,
is here with me now,
and she is also right there, where you
are, with you.

My dear Pépé,

I'm writing to you from the middle—or the beginning—of a global pandemic. You've walked through so much uncertainty, too, and faced endings you didn't choose. Tell me how to do it. You've been someone to lean on during the early months of these strange times, and with all other routes off this island closed off or banned, I've chosen to travel down this trail with you.

What would you say to us all if you could speak to us? To all of us: your grandchildren, your great-grandchildren, and your great-great-grandchildren? We aren't gathering for fiddle music; we're no longer travelling to find new homes; no longer hunting, even. What roots should we be digging at now?

Oh, Pépé—it's been years since I was able to get back to the Prairies.

The last time I was out West I sat in the grass by the river in Batoche, I stood alongside the river I skated on as a child in St. Albert, and I walked down the river in the heart of Winnipeg. All those smells surrounded me again and it brought me to my childhood. It called me back. Yes, I said on those days and in the quiet of those nights, I'll return to my homeland.

But I'll let the fireweed come up around me where I am here in St. John's. I'll tend to all the other things that are growing even in the midst of this crisis. Pépé, here I am, looking ahead and looking back.

Earlier I wrote how this word Métis was a conversation between you and I. Now it is a conversation between myself and my daughters. You left Manitoba for your daughters. I stay here in Newfoundland for mine.

I am staying put for once, letting the children grow where they sent down their roots. The time of return will come for me and I'll complete the journey. Your land will be waiting for me and for your great-great granddaughters, and the generations of women who come after.

Oh, Pépé, the books I could write about the women in the family. They deserve their own space, these women who have passed on and the ones still walking this earth. This conversation with you has led me to the feet of their stories. As this conversation between us in the pages of this book closes, the next conversation between us can finally begin.

My mama asked me not
to tell. Although I need
to set that fire and burn
I won't   I won't tell.

I'll honour that request
as far as I can.
There is more in what isn't said.
I won't tell right now all that happened
to my grandmother
or to my mother
or the rest of us. Not now.

Fires in our lives
sparked by human
activity. I must not speak it or write it
except in a broad way,
or by telling the truth in fiction.
I must hold the details in my
chest, in my belly, in my uterus.
I'll do this for now.

But it is my way to speak and to tell
I have to or I'll burn right up
And then what will my daughters
do? Motherless
except for salt and ash?

All the space here   all the space between
the words   all the short lines   all the sentences
cut off to rush ahead to the next line—in those spaces lies
        everything
I haven't written everything
I haven't said

Photo by Bojan Fürst

MICHELLE PORTER is a poet, journalist, and writer. She's a prairie Métis who moved to Newfoundland and Labrador over a decade ago—and stayed for the fog, the craggy cliffs, and the dramatic storms. Her first book of poetry, *Inquiries*, was shortlisted for the Pat Lowther Memorial Award for Best Book of Poetry, Canada 2019. Her nonfiction work has been published in journals, books, and newspapers across Canada. Her essay, *Fireweed*, was long-listed for the 2019 CBC Nonfiction Prize. She is currently the non-fiction editor with *Riddle Fence*. She is a citizen of the Métis Nation and member of the Manitoba Métis Federation.